The University in Disser

The rise of corporatism in the North American University was charted by Bill Readings in the mid-1990s in his book *The University in Ruins*. The intervening years have seen the corporate university grow and extend to the point where its evolution into a large business corporation is seemingly complete. Rolfe's book examines the factors contributing to the transformation of the university from a site of culture and knowledge to what might be termed an 'information factory', and explores strategies for how, in Readings' words, members of the academic community might continue to 'dwell in the ruins of the university' in a productive and authentic way.

Drawing on the work of critics and philosophers such as Barthes, Derrida, Lyotard and Deleuze, *The University in Dissent* suggests that this can only be achieved subversively through the development of a 'community of philosophers' who are prepared to challenge, critique and subvert the mission statement of the 'University of Excellence' from within, focusing on how scholarly and academic thought and writing might develop in this new post-Enlightenment era.

Summarising, contextualizing and extending previous understandings of the rise of corporatism and the subsequent demise of the traditional aims and values of the university, Rolfe assesses the situation in contemporary UK and international settings. He recognizes that changes to the traditional idea of the university are inevitable and explores some of the challenges and consequences of this shift in the academic world, suggesting how academics can work with change, whilst at the same time seeking to undermine its worst excesses.

This timely and thought-provoking book is a must-read for all academics at university level, as well as education policy-makers.

Gary Rolfe is Professor of Nursing in the School of Health Science, University of Swansea, UK.

The Society for Research into Higher Education (SRHE)
is an independent and financially self-supporting
international learned Society. It is concerned to advance
understanding of higher education, especially through
the insights, perspectives and knowledge offered by
systematic research and scholarship.

The Society's primary role is to improve the quality of higher education through facilitating knowledge exchange, discourse and publication of research. SRHE members are worldwide and the Society is an NGO in operational relations with UNESCO.

The Society has a wide set of aims and objectives. Amongst its many activities the Society:

• is a specialist publisher of higher education research, journals and books, amongst them Studies in Higher Education, Higher Education Quarterly, Research into Higher Education Abstracts and a long running monograph book series.

The Society also publishes a number of in-house guides and produces a specialist series "Issues in Postgraduate Education".

• funds and supports a large number of special interest networks for researchers and practitioners working in higher education from every discipline. These networks are open to all and offer a range of topical seminars, workshops and other events throughout the year ensuring the Society is in touch with all current research knowledge.

• runs the largest annual UK-based higher education research conference and parallel conference for postgraduate and newer researchers. This is attended by researchers from over 35 countries and showcases current research across every aspect of higher education.

SRHE *Society for Research into Higher Education*
Advancing knowledge Informing policy Enhancing practice

73 Collier Street
London N1 9BE
United Kingdom

T +44 (0)20 7427 2350
F +44 (0)20 7278 1135
E srheoffice@srhe.ac.uk

www.srhe.ac.uk

Director: Helen Perkins
Registered Charity No. 313850
Company No. 00868820
Limited by Guarantee
Registered office as above

Society for Research into Higher Education (SRHE) series

Series Editors: Lynn McAlpine, Oxford Learning Institute
             Jeroen Huisman, University of Bath

Published titles:

Forthcoming Titles:

The University in Dissent

Scholarship in the corporate university

Gary Rolfe

Routledge
Taylor & Francis Group

LONDON AND NEW YORK

First published 2013
by Routledge
2 Park Square, Milton Park, Abingdon, Oxon OX14 4RN together with
The Society for Research into Higher Education (SRHE)
73 Collier Street
London N1 9BE
UK

Simultaneously published in the USA and Canada
by Routledge
711 Third Avenue, New York, NY 10017 together with The Society for
Research into Higher Education(SRHE)
73 Collier Street
London N1 9BE
UK

Routledge is an imprint of the Taylor & Francis Group, an informa business

© 2013 Gary Rolfe

British Library Cataloguing in Publication Data
A catalogue record for this book is available from the British Library

Library of Congress Cataloging in Publication Data
1. Education, Higher—Aims and objectives—Great Britain. 2. Higher
education and state—Great Britain. 3. Business and education—Great
Britain. I. Title.
LB2322.2.R65 2012
378.010941—dc23
2012016348

ISBN: 978-0-415-68114-8 (hbk)
ISBN: 978-0-415-68115-5 (pbk)
ISBN: 978-0-203-08428-1 (ebk)

Typeset in Galliard
by FiSH Books Ltd, Enfield

MIX
Paper from
responsible sources
FSC
www.fsc.org   FSC® C004839

Printed and bound in Great Britain by
TJ International Ltd, Padstow, Cornwall

For Mum and Dad,
who made it all happen

Contents

Series editors' introduction

This series, co-published by the Society for Research into Higher Education and Routledge Books, aims to provide, in an accessible manner, cutting-edge scholarly thinking and inquiry that reflects the rapidly changing world of higher education, examined in a global context.

Encompassing topics of wide international relevance, the series includes every aspect of the international higher education research agenda, from strategic policy formulation and impact to pragmatic advice on best practice in the field. Each book in the series aims to meet at least one of the principal aims of the Society: to advance knowledge; to enhance practice; to inform policy.

Gary Rolfe takes us on a philosophical journey, analysing the evolution of the idea of the university. Discussing the nature of the university of the Enlightenment and lamenting the current idea of the University of Excellence, he suggests a thought-out novel idea of the Paraversity, a subversive university of Thought, which works in parallel with *and* against the corporate University of Excellence.

Lynn McAlpine
Jeroen Huisman

Preface

'At the twilight of modernity, which is also the twilight of the University as we have known it, can another way be found to think in the University?'
Bill Readings, *The University in Ruins*, 1996

When I came across Bill Readings' book, *The University in Ruins*, I must confess that it was the title that initially attracted me. It seemed to me that the university[1] (or at least *my* university), if not yet a ruin, was crumbling around me, and I was keen to read the thoughts of someone else who felt the same. I was encouraged by Readings' stated aim in his Introduction that, 'In this book I will discuss how we can reconceive the University once the story of liberal education has lost its organizing center,'[2] and by his oblique references to excellence, administration and accountancy as somehow complicit in the ruination of the university. Although written in the early 1990s from a predominantly North-American perspective, I was in little doubt before I had even begun to read the first chapter that Readings had something to say that transcended its specific time and place.

I quickly realized that I had chanced upon a remarkable book that was at once profound, insightful, scholarly and prophetic, but also obtuse, repetitive, inconclusive and (for me at least), at times, difficult to understand. Perhaps its flaws are to be expected, and are certainly to be excused, given that Readings died in tragic circumstances before he had time to complete the final draft. My reasons for writing this book therefore stem from my own struggles with Readings' brilliant yet infuriating text, and are in part a personal attempt to understand and make sense through a written engagement with it. This, after all, is the closest I am able to come to a conversation with Readings himself.

Despite being at times a difficult and even turgid read, Readings' book contains a number of highly polished gems; succinct and pithy statements that sum up perfectly my frustrations and anger with the corporate ethos in which my university is becoming ever more immersed. In particular, I recognized his description of the 'University of Excellence', 'which is not just *like* a corporation – it *is* a corporation. Students in the University of Excellence are not *like* customers, they *are* customers'.[3] Even after selling the students a degree, the University of Excellence continues to cash in with the sale of graduation T-shirts and 'logo-encrusted desk items on the Disneyland model'.[4] In order to explain his adoption of the term 'University of Excellence', Readings told the story of the Cornell University car-parking service, which was given an award for 'excellence in parking' in recognition of the fact 'that they had achieved a remarkable level of efficiency in *restricting* motor vehicle access'.[5] Although ironic and somewhat amusing in itself, Readings used this story to demonstrate the empty nature of the concept of excellence. He pointed out that the term 'excellent' could just as easily be applied to attempts to increase *or* decrease the number of parking spaces available to faculty, so that 'excellence can function equally well as an evaluative criterion on either side of the issue of what constitutes "excellence in parking"'.[6] This notion of excellence as an empty referent, a term devoid of meaning that can be used to 'talk up' almost anything, emerges periodically as a key concept throughout his book.

Readings' responses to the corporate madness of the University of Excellence are both radical and often amusing. For example, he proposed that vice chancellors should be made to write 'student essays' to evaluate their universities rather than 'elaborate banal and cliché-ridden mission statements (which are all the same from university to university) and then quantify how far they have lived up to them'.[7] As he observed, 'on the one hand, they all claim that theirs is a unique educational institution. On the other hand, they all go on to describe this uniqueness in exactly the same way.'[8]

Perhaps these incisive and acerbic observations were only to be expected from a writer who had previously defined the American university as a loose association of people united by a common interest in parking (or the lack of it!). However, it would be very wrong to think that Readings' point was simply, as one of the reviewers on the back cover of his book misleadingly put it, 'that corporate-style management has become part of the fabric of university administration'.[9] For Readings, the turn to managerialism was not so much a *cause* as a *consequence* of a far deeper and more profound shift in society, culture and the nation-state. As such, the ruination of the university cannot be reversed or even resisted. The best we can do is to learn to dwell in the ruins without recourse to nostalgia or romanticism.

Readings began to address this task in the final chapters of his book, but his conclusions were (perhaps deliberately) tentative. His words at the end of the last chapter appear to be written hurriedly in an abbreviated note-style:

> That a major shift in the role and function of the intellectual is occurring is clear. What it will come to have meant is an issue upon which those in the University should attempt to have an impact. An attention to this problematic is necessary. How we pay attention to it is not determined.

Therein lies both the freedom and the enormous responsibility of Thought at the end of the twentieth century, which is also the end of what has been the epoch of the nation-state.[10]

This, then, is the challenge bequeathed to us by Bill Readings, a challenge that becomes more urgent with every day that passes.

Acknowledgements

'Scholarship is a choice of how to live as well as a choice of career.'
C. Wright Mills, *On Intellectual Craftsmanship*, 1959

In writing this book I have drawn on 40 years of experiences in higher education, initially as a student and latterly as an academic. It therefore seems fitting to acknowledge the generosity, kindness, help and support given to me at all stages of my scholarly adventure. Thanks, then, to my mum and dad who, as far back as I can remember, encouraged, cajoled and did everything possible to ensure that I was the first person from my family to go to university.

Thanks also to friends and colleagues (too numerous to mention) from various stages of my career for support and mentorship, and for showing me the power of creative thought and action. In particular, Dave Carpenter and Ian McRae, senior colleagues and role models from my early career in Portsmouth; Phil Barker, who never ceases to inspire and stimulate me; and Martin Johnson for being a critical friend and valued colleague.

More specifically, I have to thank the anonymous reviewers who recommended the publication of this book, and Philip Mudd and the team at Routledge Education for taking a chance with it. Thanks also to Ruth Davies at Swansea University for reading a draft version and providing helpful and encouraging feedback.

Finally, I wish to express my deep indebtedness and love to my wife, colleague and (critical) friend, Lyn Gardner, for 30 years of practical, emotional and intellectual support, for her honest and unerringly accurate feedback and critique, and for always being there; and, of course, my three sons, Gabby, Jude and Jack, for pretending not to notice all the times when my head (and sometimes the rest of me) was elsewhere.

Part I

The ruined university

'The scholar disappears. He is succeeded by the research man who is engaged in research projects. These, rather than the cultivation of erudition, lend to his work its atmosphere of incisiveness. The research man no longer needs a library at home. Moreover, he is constantly on the move. He negotiates at meetings and collects information at congresses. He contracts for commissions with publishers. The latter now determine along with him which books must be written.'

Martin Heidegger, *The Age of the World Picture*, 1938

The disappearance of the scholar from our universities, to be replaced by the 'research man', was foreseen and foretold by Martin Heidegger in the 1930s. Heidegger's research man, in effect a corporate worker in a corporate business whose job is to bid for and negotiate contracts for the collection and dissemination of information, was described in detail 60 years later by Bill Readings. The difference, however, was that whereas Heidegger was warning us of what might happen to the university and those who work in it if we did not check the rise of scientific instrumentalism, Readings was surveying the ruins caused by the abandonment of 'the cultivation of erudition' for the production of information.

In Part 1 of this book, I attempt to summarize, contextualize and extend Readings' important and timely thesis of the rise of corporatism and the subsequent demise of the traditional intentions and values of scholarship, bringing his ideas up to date and applying them to the contemporary UK and international setting. Readings' conclusion is that in order to save the university as an academic institution, it is necessary to challenge the 'idea of excellence' and replace it with 'the name of Thought'. Building on Readings' thesis, I suggest that this can only be achieved subversively through the development of a community of philosophers that is prepared to challenge and critique the mission statement of the 'University of Excellence' from within.

In light of the unfinished nature of *The University in Ruins*, I have set myself three broad aims. First, to simplify and explicate the content, and to try to relate it explicitly to my own experiences in a UK university in the twenty-first century. Second, to attempt to impose a more or less linear narrative structure on a somewhat circular (or perhaps circuitous) account in which arguments are repeated, restated and revisited from chapter to chapter. Whilst this might have been a deliberate stylistic decision by Readings, it is more likely to be due to the fact that many of the chapters are modified from previously published journal papers, and I suspect that much of this repetition would have been edited out of the final polished draft. Third, and most challengingly, I have attempted to extend Readings' thesis beyond the point he had reached when his thinking and writing was cruelly and prematurely terminated. That is not to say that I have anticipated where Readings might have taken his lines of reasoning, but rather that I have used his arguments to further my own ends and my own interests, for which I hope he would have forgiven me.

The content of Part 1 therefore overlaps to some extent with Readings' own book, and I make no apologies for the liberal use of quotations from *The University in Ruins*, preferring in general to allow Readings to make his own points in his own words. It also mirrors the overall structure of Readings' book, which can be divided broadly into three sections. In Chapter 1, I outline the problem of the ruined university and attempt to engage with some of the concepts and terminology introduced by Readings in the opening chapters of his book, including his notions of culture, excellence, administration and the post-historical university, in order to explore and explain the woeful situation in which we currently find ourselves. In Chapter 2, I tackle the theme of Readings' central chapters in which he charts the history of the modern university and, in particular, the rise and fall of philosophy, literature and, latterly, cultural studies as its 'master discipline'. At the end of Chapter 2, I begin to identify a way forward, a way in which we might dwell in the ruins of the university 'after excellence' without recourse, in Readings' words, either to militant radicalism or cynical despair. Although Readings begins this task in his final two chapters, he offers only a tantalizing glimpse of what might be built in the ruins of the University of Excellence. I therefore attempt to push beyond the explicit content of Readings' book to speculate on and develop further some of his uncompleted and half-theorized concepts and injunctions, which I frame within the idea of the 'Paraversity' as an invisible, subversive, virtual institution that exists alongside the ruined university.

Chapter 1

The academy in peril

'Every thinker puts some portion of an apparently stable world in peril.'
John Dewey, *Experience and Nature*, 1929

Introduction

Anyone who has worked or studied for any length of time in higher education over the past two decades cannot fail to have noticed a number of dramatic changes across every aspect of the university. Although these changes have been many and diverse, they are generally regarded either as the *impetus for* or as the *result of* a growing corporatism and managerialism, to the extent that universities are now being organised and run as major business players in the increasingly lucrative 'knowledge economy'.[1] In what Frank Furedi describes as 'the age-old tension between economic calculation and a commitment to impersonal and non-instrumental values such as the advancement of knowledge and science',[2] it would appear that economic calculation has emerged on top. Supporters of these developments regard them as necessary responses to changes in how the university is funded (particularly the need to attract more 'paying customers'); to the emergence of new academic disciplines (and the demise of long-established ones) in response to the demands from these paying customers for vocational courses; and to the growing need for management, administration and accountancy in an ever larger and more complex organisation. Academics and students alike are being told that the university can no longer afford them the time for unproductive speculative thinking, that they must engage with the 'real world' of finance and industry, and, increasingly, that academics must justify their existence in terms of research grants from external funding organisations.

Responses from within the academy to these changes and challenges tend to follow one of two broad themes. On the one hand are those who rail against recent moves to corporatise the university by advocating a return to 'the good old days' and a rebuilding of the ivory towers. On the other hand are those who seek to adapt and profit from the new regime, who reason that they are powerless to bring about a return to the way things used to be, or else who argue that it is only right that universities (and individuals within them) should compete for customers and funding with other private and public-sector organizations in a global market economy.

In his book *The University in Ruins*, the academic, literary theorist and writer Bill Readings sets out an alternative vision for the university that argues neither for the necessity and inevitability of the current project of (as he sees it) the ruination of the university, nor for the romantic and largely untenable project of rebuilding from the ruins. Rather, he asserts:

> I want to perform a structural diagnosis of contemporary shifts in the University's function as an institution in order to argue that the wider social role of the University as an institution is now up for grabs.[3]

Readings' project, and mine, is a 'structural diagnosis' of the modern university and its engagement with the cultural life of western society over the past 200 years.[4] Readings sets out to demonstrate how the rationale and purpose of the university has shifted during this time from 'reason' to 'culture' and eventually to what he calls 'excellence',[5] and how this shift has resulted in the current 'crisis of legitimation' with regard to the role and function of universities and those who teach and study in them. However, the aim of this diagnosis is not merely to chart the history of the ruined university, nor to bemoan our current plight as small cogs in a large business organization, but rather, as Readings points out, to argue that the university as an institution is now 'up for grabs', and to explore and expound a strategy for grabbing it.

The rise and fall of the modern university

Readings begins his structural diagnosis with the origins of the modern university in Berlin at the start of the nineteenth century. The foundations of the modern university were first expounded by the philosopher Friedrich Schleiermacher and later enacted by the Prussian minister of education Karl Wilhelm von Humboldt, and were based on a belief in the intrinsic value of intellectual inquiry and the Enlightenment aspiration to 'lay open the whole body of learning and expound both the principles and foundations of all knowledge'.[6]

The modern university thus emerged as an important component of the Enlightenment project of universal knowledge and progress through science and reason, which Readings calls 'the historical project of culture'.[7] Readings defines culture as, on the one hand, the unity of all knowledges that are the object of study, and, on the other hand, the process of development or cultivation of character.[8] Culture can therefore be seen as 'the symbolic and political counterpart to the project of integration pursued by the nation-state',[9] that is as the social glue of national identity. As a major player in the project of national culture, the early development of the modern university was closely linked to the emergence of the various western European nation-states and took on different characteristics in Germany, France, Scotland and England (and, later, the USA and Canada). However, Readings claims that the modern university was not merely a *product* of the Enlightenment, but that it also played a central role in *maintaining* the Enlightenment project by producing and disseminating the cultural norms, values and aspirations of the nation-state. Drawing on the work of the French philosopher Jean-François Lyotard, Readings argues that the modern university in western Europe both sustained and was sustained by national culture. In particular, he suggests that the Enlightenment grand narratives of truth and emancipa-tion[10] not only defined the subject matter of the university but also acted as its 'narratives of legitimation',[11] its organizing principles and terms of refer-ence.

The Enlightenment grand narratives of truth and emancipation were set in opposition at the birth of the modern university at the turn of the nine-teenth century and have been in a state of conflict ever since. As we have seen, the modern university was founded on the principles of German ideal-ism, that is on the pursuit of knowledge for its own sake, with truth as the ultimate goal of academic inquiry. However, although this idealist philoso-phy emerged as the blueprint for the modern university, there also existed at the time a contrasting vision of the Napoleonic university, which arose following the French Revolution. Rather than a community of self-govern-ing scholars pursuing knowledge for its own sake, this alternative model brought the university firmly under state control and was driven by the revo-lutionary ideal that knowledge should be controlled by the state and put to work for the good of society. However, the project ultimately failed, and Lyotard notes that this 'humanist principle that humanity rises up in dignity and freedom through knowledge [was] left by the wayside'.[12] Thus, for more than a century, the university was guided and legitimated by the idealist narrative of truth rather than the utilitarian narrative of emancipation.

This Enlightenment grand narrative of truth resonated with the nineteenth-century Romantic vision in which 'Beauty is truth, truth beauty',[13] and tended to favour the project of the arts rather than the sciences at a time when the term 'science' was only just entering general circulation in the university, and where science was usually subsumed under the liberal arts. Since the time of the Ancient Greeks, the project of the arts has been to distinguish between appearance and essence and to pursue the latter. In Aristotle's words, 'the aim of art is to represent not the outward appearance of things, but their inward significance'.[14] More than 2,000 years later, we find the same sentiments echoed in the words of the architect Frank Lloyd Wright, for whom 'the truth is more important than the facts'. Art is (or should be) concerned not with how things seem (the facts), but with how they really are (the truth).[15] Indeed, the fact of the matter, the outward appearance, is of little interest to the artist, who wishes to capture the essence, the soul, of what she sees before her. This concern with *essence*, arguably, applies across the entire spectrum of artistic endeavour from painting and poetry to photography and drama; in each case the aim is to penetrate or transcend the mundane world of outward appearance to represent things *as they really are*.

However, in recent years Lyotard has noted that the second Enlightenment grand narrative of emancipation has been 'gaining new vigour',[16] and is associated with the rise of the concept of the self-managing autonomous subject. This utilitarian view, which regards knowledge as the means to the ends of freedom, justice and the reduction of suffering, is nowadays most often found in university departments of natural, biological, social and political sciences. The rationale for this scientific narrative in which 'knowledge is no longer the subject, but in the service of the subject',[17] is technological control, which in turn results in freedom and emancipation from the blind and often hostile forces of nature. This grand narrative usually takes a realist or neorealist view in which truth is defined in terms of a correspondence to the external, empirical, 'real' world of facts, and regards the purpose of science as *Erklären* (explanation) rather than *Verstehen* (understanding). As Auguste Comte, the nineteenth-century advocate of 'a positive science of society', observes:

> Finally, in the positive state, the human mind, *recognizing the impossibility of obtaining absolute truth*, gives up the search after the origin and hidden causes of the universe and a knowledge of the final causes of phenomena. It endeavours now only to discover, by a well-combined use of reasoning and observation, the actual laws of phenomena... The explanation of facts, thus reduced to its real terms, consists henceforth only in the connection established between different particular phenomena and some general facts, the number of which the progress of science tends more and more to diminish.[18]

Thus, whereas in the arts absolute truth or essence is more important than 'mere facts', scientists, including social scientists, have traditionally argued against the notion of absolute truth in favour of a form of surface or factual truth; that in a sense, the observable facts *are* the truth, or at least, as close as we can come to it.[19]

As we have seen, these grand narratives have always existed in a state of tension and conflict, perhaps best exemplified by the public and acrimonious 'two cultures' debate in the 1950s and 1960s between C.P. Snow (on the side of science) and F.R. Leavis (on the side of literature and the arts). Snow's point is that since the Renaissance, the arts and the sciences have become more and more separated until we have reached a point where the two cultures do not, and indeed cannot, talk to each other.[20] Snow lays much of the blame at the feet of what he referred to as the 'literary intellectuals', claiming that whereas many scientists took an interest in the arts (Snow himself was a published novelist), most academic members of arts faculties were 'natural Luddites' who displayed a staggering lack of knowledge about even what Snow regarded as the 'first principles' of science such as the laws of thermodynamics.[21]

The project of the modern university can be seen as an attempt to reunite these disparate 'two cultures', to demonstrate how aesthetics and empirics, the inner and the outer, the truth and the facts, complement one another and form a whole that is at once *unifying* and *universal*. This very difficult, perhaps impossible, task of maintaining and uniting these two grand narratives of science and the arts has, traditionally, fallen to the discipline of philosophy, which Schleiermacher regarded as the space where knowledge may reflect on itself and which Kant saw as the seat of reason within the university. However, Readings suggests that Snow's 'culture wars' were triggered by 'the invention of the category of literature' and the subsequent 'move from philosophy to literary studies as the major discipline entrusted by the nation-state with the task of reflecting on cultural identity'.[22] The problem, as Readings sees it, was that whereas the discipline of philosophy understood and mediated between the arts and the sciences, 'the literary is opposed to the scientific in a way philosophy is not'.[23] This discussion about the location of the 'cultural heart' of the university will be resumed and expanded later in the book. As we shall see, a major part of Lyotard's project is to restore philosophy (albeit in a rather different guise) to its traditional and rightful place at the centre of the university.[24]

We have seen that, for Readings, the production and dissemination of culture has been 'the legitimating idea of the modern University', its *raison d'être*. However, he continues, 'the nation-state and the modern notion of culture arose together, and they are, I argue, ceasing to be essential to an increasingly transnational global economy'.[25] Not only is culture at war with itself, but the importance of culture as a unifying activity in our national life is also in decline, and with it the defining role of the university as an institution dedicated to safeguarding and propagating national culture.[26] Lyotard links this questioning of the purpose of the university to a wider postmodern incredulity towards grand narratives in general, and to the Enlightenment grand narratives of truth and emancipation in particular. For Lyotard, the ultimate failure of modernism was exemplified by the events at Auschwitz, which pushed the Enlightenment cultural ideals of reason and rationality to their logical and perhaps inevitable conclusion: the scientific and rational administration of genocide. As Readings notes: 'the summit of reason, order, administration, is also the summit of terror'.[27] We might argue that 'after Auschwitz',[28] western society felt that it could no longer trust itself, and has instead handed over responsibility for its management and development to the impersonal forces of economics and the market. Thus the twin cultural pillars of the Enlightenment university are crumbling and the grand narratives of truth and emancipation have been replaced by the monolith of liberal capitalism; culture has been superseded by economics as the driving force of the university.[29]

The University of Excellence

The diminishing role and status of Enlightenment culture during the second half of the twentieth century has brought about a crisis of legitimation for the modern university, which has been forced to respond to the challenges of the postmodern age.[30] However, whereas a postmodern stance would suggest, in Lyotard's words, an incredulity towards *all* grand narratives, the university has merely replaced the Enlightenment grand narratives of truth and emancipation with an unquestioning acceptance of the liberal capitalist grand narrative of the market.[31] For this reason, Readings is reluctant to refer to the 'postmodern university', since there has been little or no attempt to embrace the postmodern values of scepticism and anti-foundationalism. He also argues that, in any case, the label 'postmodern' is commonly misunderstood to refer simply to that which follows on from modernism. As he points out, there is a danger that we might end up speaking about the postmodern university as if it were 'a newer, more critical institution, which is to say, *an even more modern* University than the modern University'.[32] He continues:

> I would prefer to call the contemporary University 'posthistorical' rather than 'postmodern' in order to insist upon the sense that the institution has outlived itself, is now a survivor of the era in which it defined itself in terms of the project of the *historical* development, affirmation, and inculcation of national culture.[33]

Readings suggests that the production and dissemination of culture has been replaced in the post-historical university by the pursuit of excellence as its 'legitimating idea', with the Enlightenment grand narratives of truth and emancipation being superseded by the liberal capitalist grand narratives of efficiency and profitability. Furthermore, whereas the production and dissemination of culture was achieved in the Enlightenment university through research and teaching, excellence is ensured through administration. For Readings, the promotion of the business values of excellence, administration, efficiency and profitability spell the ruin of the university as an academic institution.

Excellence

On the face of it, the pursuit of excellence might appear to be a noble aim and a sound principle of legitimation, and the idea of the 'University of Excellence' might appear to be almost tautological. However, Readings makes the point that, unlike culture, 'excellence' is in itself an empty signifier bereft of any ideological intent, a unit of measurement rather than something to be measured. The concept of excellence can therefore be applied to justify almost any aim. For example, an excellent course might be defined by an academic as one that has very high standards that many students fail to reach, or, conversely, it might be defined by an administrator as a course with a very low attrition rate that retains most of its students.

In order for excellence to function, it needs to be operationalized in terms of a quality or quantity. The University of Excellence has generally opted for the latter approach, and defines excellence in numerical terms. Thus, excellence in teaching is often measured by the number of first-class degrees awarded to students or by their attrition rate, and excellence in research is determined by the amount of grant income obtained or the output of published papers. This view of excellence as a *quantity* rather than a *quality* brings it into the realm of efficiency, profitability and administration.

However, as soon as quantity becomes more important than quality; as soon as universities are judged according to the number of students who obtain good degrees (where 'good' is defined numerically as a 'first' or an 'upper second') rather than the quality of the educational experience; according to the numbers of papers published in journals with high 'impact factors' (that is with large numbers of citations) rather than according to the quality of those papers; as soon as outcome becomes more important than process; then the principles of the Enlightenment are undermined and the entire edifice of the university begins to teeter. The aspiration towards excellence, seen in the mission statements of so many universities,[34] can only be demonstrated through a crude quantification of targets that is the very antithesis of the quality to which these universities previously aspired.

Administration

Perhaps even more worrying, Readings suggests that, in the 'bureaucratic corporation' that the university has become, administration has taken over from research and teaching as the means by which excellence is to be delivered. This is only to be expected, since whereas the concern with culture focuses on the *content* of what is to be researched and taught, the excellence agenda is more concerned with defining, operationalizing, measuring and comparing the *standards* of researching and teaching. Thus 'excellence names a non-referential principle that allows the maximum of uninterrupted internal administration'.[35]

Readings' thesis that the administration of excellence has replaced the dissemination of culture as the prime concern of the university is best demonstrated by examining what counts as quality in teaching. Readings tells of how, in 1993, a Canadian weekly news magazine attempted to rank all universities in Canada using its 'measure of excellence', which quantified teaching in terms of student–teacher ratio, the numbers of lecturers with PhDs, and so on. When Teaching Quality Assessment (TQA) was first introduced in the UK in the 1990s, it relied upon a very similar crude form of quantification of excellence, where points were awarded for such numerical targets as time taken for the student to progress through the system, student retention rates, course completion rates and graduate employment data. The implication was that the excellent lecturer was one who efficiently administered the student through the system in such a way that facilitated the 'quality' targets of the university. It could be argued then that Teaching Quality Assessment was concerned little with either teaching or quality, but rather with administration and quantity.

In recent years, TQA has been replaced in England by institutional self-evaluation under the auspices of the Quality Assurance Agency (QAA), which is responsible for ensuring that mechanisms and procedures are in place for each university to monitor and assess its own quality. As the change in title suggests, the remit of the agency has shifted from the direct *assessment* of teaching quality to the indirect *assurance* of general quality and standards through the monitoring of the systems and structures in place in each institution. The QAA describes its quality assurance role as follows:

> Institutional review addresses the ultimate responsibility for the management of quality and standards that rests with the institution as a whole. It is concerned particularly with the way an institution exercises its powers as a body able to grant degrees and/or other awards. It results in reports on the degree of confidence that may reasonably be placed in an institution's effectiveness in managing the academic standards of its awards and the quality of its programmes.[36]

Educational excellence is therefore achieved and demonstrated through the effective *management* or *administration* of quality and standards rather than by directly attempting to assess quality itself. Institutional review is concerned, for example, with an examination of *procedures* put in place by the organisation for the review of academic programmes rather than with the actual programmes, and with *management* of student assessment *processes* rather than directly with student assessment. There has clearly been a shift in focus and responsibility for the delivery and assessment of excellence in teaching from the academic to the administrator. The delivery of excellence has been replaced by the administration of excellence, where excellence is itself defined in terms of quantity rather than quality.

Efficiency and profitability

The advent of the liberal-capitalist University of Excellence has also witnessed the introduction of market values into the education system, not least in that undergraduate education in England and Wales is no longer free at the point of delivery. This has, without doubt, had an effect on attitudes of undergraduate students, who are far more aware that they are, in a sense, customers with consumer rights and expectations about what they are purchasing. When they pay to enrol on a course, it is possible that many students do not wish to purchase the educational experience and some do not even wish to exchange their cash for the knowledge identified in the learning outcomes; they are mainly interested in the academic credits awarded on successful completion. This assertion will be further examined later in the chapter in relation to the knowledge economy.

The research agenda of the university has also become inextricably linked to finance and profit. Whereas external grants have always been important as a source of funding for research projects, the Research Assessment Exercise (RAE), introduced into the UK in the early 1990s,[37] elevated grant income to one of the major indicators of quality. Along with the impact factor of the journals in which research papers are published, the quality of the research conducted by an academic department is measured by the amount of grant income awarded. This has led to a situation where academics feel compelled to take on projects *not* because they have a particular interest or expertise in the subject or methodology, not even necessarily because their university might make some money out of the project, but primarily because, in the post-historical bureaucratic corporation that the university has become, grant income is a major criterion used to assess research quality, and excellence is therefore, to some extent, measured by profit margins, much as it would be in any corporate business.[38]

The pressure to compete for multi-million pound research grants has necessitated the formation of large multidisciplinary research teams that resemble Fordist production lines, where each member has a small, specialised job and rarely gets to see the big picture. Academic research has become a technology, an information machine driven by the ethos of efficiency and administration rather than intellectual craftsmanship, the desire for knowledge and the building and testing of theory.[39] The university is therefore moving away from the values of the academy towards the rules and rigours of manufacturing industry and the production line. Emphasis is increasingly on throughput rather than process, on research funding *in* and research papers *out*, and on quantitative measures of quality and 'excellence'.

The knowledge economy

It could be argued that the corporate University of Excellence is simply a logical response to what Drucker[40] has referred to as the knowledge economy. In its original form, Drucker's thesis refers to a post-industrial shift away from manufacturing towards the service industries. This shift can be seen quite readily in the University of Excellence, where many of the 'pure' disciplines and subject areas have been replaced by various 'applied' courses ending in the word 'studies,'[41] which take a 'pick-and-mix' approach to traditional arts and science subjects and which have their sights set firmly on the graduate employment market. However, the knowledge economy also refers to the growing importance of knowledge as a commodity, and this shift clearly has implications for universities, pulling them away from the 'culture business' of the Enlightenment project, and even away from the 'education business', and locating them firmly in the 'business business'. As Robin Usher points out: 'If knowledge is the currency of the new economy, universities are inevitably involved in its production.'[42]

Inevitably, the adoption of market values at the very core of the university has been at the cost of traditional academic activities with less tangible outcomes that cannot be exchanged or bartered in the knowledge economy. In a climate where Drucker's equation of knowledge with finance has been taken to its (il)logical conclusion, wisdom has (to paraphrase T.S. Eliot) been replaced in importance by knowledge, and knowledge has subsequently been replaced by information as the most flexible and liquid currency of the academy. The effects of this shift in values can be seen both in the teaching and the research missions of the University of Excellence.

Teaching and the knowledge economy

Teaching has traditionally been considered the core function of the university, at least in the UK. The mediaeval university was established to provide training for the Church and the professions, and the focus on teaching was retained in the early Modern Universities of the nineteenth century. This is certainly the sentiment expressed by John Henry Newman in his book *The Idea of a University*, published in the 1850s, where he claims, in the opening sentence of the Preface, that a university is:

> a place of *teaching* universal *knowledge*. This implies that its object is, on the one hand, intellectual, not moral; and, on the other, that it is the diffusion and extension of knowledge rather than the advancement.[43]

Gordon Graham has argued that, with a handful of exceptions, this focus on diffusion rather than extension of knowledge has continued to the present day, and that 'British universities exist, in large measure, to educate those who register in them as students, and depend heavily upon the support of the public purse as the provider of university education.'[44] However, this view would be regarded by many contemporary writers as somewhat eccentric, and it is widely accepted that the postwar years, from 1945 to the mid-1970s, saw 'an important shift away from teaching and towards research', to the extent that 'knowledge itself was seen as the primary product of higher education, not students'.[45] We have already seen that the market for knowledge is being replaced by a need and desire for unprocessed information, and even, in an age where information becomes out-of-date at a rapid rate, for the ability to *generate* information; that is, for empirical data-collection skills.[46] This shift in market demand from knowledge to information, to information generation has been accompanied by a shift in the educational remit of the academic from teaching to learning, to learning to learn.

In fact, there is nothing new about the modern educational focus on 'learning-to-learn'. As Readings points out, the German philosopher Johann Gottlieb Fichte claimed in 1807 that the purpose of university education is not to transmit information but to encourage critical judgement: 'What is thus taught is not facts but critique – the formal art of the use of mental powers, the process of judgement.'[47] However, it could be argued that the University of Excellence has 'bought in' to the learning-to-learn agenda for political and economic, rather than pedagogic, reasons. On the one hand, it gives the impression of an institution at the cutting edge of educational technology, where students are 'self-directed' and classrooms are 'virtual', and where learning is controlled and organized by individual students to suit their own needs. On the other hand, student-directed learning has the added benefit of allowing academics additional time to pursue the more profitable and more highly regarded activity of research.

This somewhat corrupted version of self-directed learning calls to mind George Ritzer's thesis of 'McDonaldization'.[48] For Ritzer, the masterstroke of the McDonald's restaurant chain was its success in persuading customers to act as their own waiters and even to clear up their own mess. From the perspective of McDonaldization, the self-teaching student is merely an extension of the self-serving customer. Another key component of McDonaldization that we might wish to consider in relation to the teaching mission of the University of Excellence is the redefining of excellence in terms of a *consistent* and *reliable* product, even if that product is, in fact, mediocre in quality. Thus, for McDonald's, an excellent burger is one that tastes exactly like one bought at any other McDonald's restaurant anywhere else in the world, rather than a burger that tastes better than those offered by their competitors. Similarly, internal consistency is becoming the major criterion for judging the quality of university teaching. It is, of course, tempting to apply Ritzer's thesis to other aspects of the University of Excellence such as 'self-auditing', where the university does the job of the external auditors and where it is possible to meet mediocre and educationally insignificant 'standards' in an excellent way.

We might expect, therefore, that the students' perspective of what is on offer in the University of Excellence is somewhat at odds with the mission statement of the promotion of excellence. As we have seen, the focus on self-directed learning, coupled with the introduction into English and Welsh universities of the up-front payment of fees, has called into question just what it is that students are paying for. In a situation where most university courses have been modularized and each module allocated CATS points,[49] it is tempting for students to regard universities as little more than *bureaux des changes*, or what Zygmunt Bauman refers to as 'credentials and certifying agencies',[50] where they are able to exchange their fees for academic credits that can later be converted into hard cash in the form of access to paid employment. As Bauman points out, 'It is the universities, after all, who remain the sole institutions entitled to encrust the individual know-how with public validity, and thus with an exchange value.'[51] Such a situation has benefits for the university as well as for the student, since most university departments have almost unlimited CATS points at their disposal but very little hard cash.

Research and the knowledge economy

Ernest Boyer, in bemoaning the decline of scholarship in north America, points out that research is a recent but rapidly developing activity in the university, and that the term did not in fact enter the vocabulary of higher education until the 1870s in the UK, and 1906 in the USA.[52] Whilst this might well be true, it is somewhat naive to suppose that it is research itself, rather than the word, that has only recently become a component of academic activity. Thus, Newman in the mid-nineteenth century refers to 'scientific and philosophical discovery' in place of research; and prior to Newman, before the term 'science' took on its current empirical experimental meaning,[53] researchers were referred to as 'natural philosophers'. It could be argued, then, that what Boyer is actually objecting to is the rise in importance of a particular *type* of research, of empirical scientific experimentation in place of older notions of scholarly intellectual inquiry.

Another way of looking at this distinction is to differentiate between 'pure' and 'applied' research. Graham makes the case that 'pure science is not the acquisition of *knowledge* for its own sake, but rather the pursuit of *understanding*'.[54] This might well be the case, but we saw previously how the early positivist social science researchers eschewed understanding (*Verstehen*) in favour of a far more pragmatic and applied emphasis on explanation (*Erklären*), that is on the generation of empirical facts and the establishment of scientific laws. Whilst Graham argues convincingly that the product of pure research (enrichment) is no less valuable than the output of applied research (usefulness), he also points out that there is an unfortunate tendency to confuse enrichment with prosperity and therefore to judge pure research by the wrong criterion.

Perhaps partly as a result of this confusion, the shift towards a corporate business ethos in higher education in the years following the Second World

War has played a large part in the demise of pure research and non-empirical scholarly activity and the corresponding growth and importance of applied scientific research as the dominant activity in the University of Excellence. Certainly, the knowledge economy has demanded a shift, in Newman's words, from the 'diffusion' to the 'advancement' of knowledge, and if the corporate university is now expected to be productive, then research-based empirical knowledge and information would seem to be the obvious output.[55]

In a setting where the generation of research findings is driven by economic demands as much as by the desire for the 'advancement of knowledge' and where output is valued more than process, we might expect there to be a growing emphasis on the writing and publication of research papers as a key indicator of production. As early as 1963, the bio-scientist Bernard Forscher wrote a letter to the journal *Science* in the form of a parable or cautionary tale in which he compared researchers to brickmakers and theorists to builders 'who constructed edifices, called explanations or laws, by assembling bricks, called facts'. He concluded:

> The brickmakers became obsessed with the making of bricks. When reminded that the ultimate goal was edifices, not bricks, they replied that, if enough bricks were available, the builders would be able to select what was necessary and still continue to construct edifices. It became difficult to complete a useful edifice because, as soon as the foundations were discernable, they were buried under an avalanche of random bricks. And, saddest of all, sometimes no effort was made even to maintain the distinction between a pile of bricks and a true edifice.[56]

Forscher's point was clear: he felt that the production and publication of research findings was taking precedence over using those findings to develop the nascent discipline of bio-science, and that any possibility of constructive development was 'being buried under an avalanche of random bricks'; indeed, that piles of bricks (research findings) were being mistaken for actual buildings (the construction of knowledge and theory). In the intervening years, the situation has become far worse, and much of the blame (at least in the UK) can be laid at the feet of the series of Research Assessment Exercises (RAEs) conducted since the early 1990s. Arguably, scores obtained in the RAE have come to be seen as the defining criterion of academic quality, resulting in disproportionate value being placed by the academy on brickmakers (empirical researchers) at the expense of architects and builders (theorists and scholars).

Other effects of this turn to research have been a rampant, but very conservative, journal-publishing industry, resulting in an unbalanced and, arguably, unhealthy state of affairs in which not only we have more research findings than we know what to do with, but perhaps even more pernicious and dangerous, the values and standards of the research laboratory take precedence over those of the academy, to the extent that many believe that the values of the laboratory *are* the values of the academy. For example, the application of 'rigour' is seen as extremely important in experimental scientific research, where the precise and rigid application of method is rightly regarded as an essential guarantor of reliability. However, it is now common to invoke the concept of rigour when making judgements about scholarly work of *all* kinds, so that rigidity, inflexibility and the blind and unswerving application of method are coming to be seen as more important qualities in an academic than flexibility, reflexivity and independent judgement.[57]

The imposition of the values and rules of science on the academy as a whole is sometimes referred to as scientism, which has been defined as 'the belief that science, especially natural science, is much the most valuable part of human learning – much the most valuable part because it is much the most authoritative, or serious, or beneficial'.[58] The German critical theorist Theodor Adorno had previously presented a more extreme version of this argument by claiming that the method of science has become not merely the *most authoritative* route to knowledge and truth, but the *only* route. Thus:

> the appeal to science, the rules by which it functions, the absolute validity of the methods to which it owes its development, together constitute an authority which penalises free, untrammelled, 'untrained' thinking and will not allow the minds of men to dwell on matters that do not bear the stamp of its approval.[59]

This, in turn, prompted Jürgen Habermas to define scientism as 'the conviction that we can no longer understand science as one form of possible knowledge, but rather must identify knowledge with science'.[60]

Habermas's fear that all knowledge has come to be defined in terms of science and the scientific method is borne out in the thesis put forward by the medical doctor Raymond Tallis.[61] Tallis begins with the introduction into medicine in the 1940s of the double-blind randomised controlled trial as 'the only truly robust method for obtaining good evidence', and then attempts to argue that a similar approach to gathering evidence should be employed throughout the arts and humanities. It is, perhaps, instructive to quote him at length:

> The lack of appropriate quantitative methods to acquire the data necessary to underpin descriptive general statements and to ensure the validity of causal explanations... lies at the heart of the present crisis in the humanities. In an age in which it is increasingly expected that general statements should be supported by robust evidence if they are to command credence, the humanities are in danger of being simply

anachronistic, acceptable only to arts graduates who have known no better and are unacquainted with adequate methodological discipline.[62]

But, as Tallis points out, there can be no such 'robust evidence' for many arts and humanities disciplines, and even where the possibility exists, for example in 'cultural history', the cost and trouble of acquiring such data would preclude their collection. Thus, in contrast to 'the cautious clinical scientist', Tallis asks, 'Why [in the humanities] are the quacks – with their instant diagnoses and instant cures – in the ascendant? Why does being a rotten scholar peddling exciting ideas attract tenure rather than scandal?'.[63] Ultimately, then:

> large-scale empirical statements – such as are made by many cultural theorists and historians – have to be underpinned by properly designed large-scale empirical enquiries...If one does not have the means to acquire the data to support higher-level generalisations, one should avoid them. In short, if you can't substantiate statements, don't make them.[64]

If Einstein had adhered to this principle, his revolutionary thought experiments on relativity would never have been published. If taken to the extreme, Tallis's injunction would rule out entire disciplinary fields such as theoretical physics and literary studies. Whilst Tallis's equation of non-empirical speculation with 'rotten scholarship' is at best sensationalist and at worst patent nonsense, it nevertheless provides an extremely graphic example of the way that the values, standards and attitudes of laboratory science have come to impose on the academy as a whole.

The demise of scholarship

This colonization of the academy by science and scientists was first noted by Martin Heidegger during the 1930s. He pointed out that science was coming to be defined purely in terms of research, that research was in turn defined as rigorous adherence to methodology, and that methodology was constantly adapting to technological advances in data-collection methods. Ultimately, he predicted, the institution of the university would become defined by and subservient to the demands of science as research, and those who work in universities would be shaped and moulded by the same demands.

> Hence the decisive development of the modern character of science as ongoing activity also forms men of a different stamp. *The scholar disappears*. He is succeeded by the research man who is engaged in research projects. These, rather than the cultivation of erudition, lend to his work

its atmosphere of incisiveness. The research man no longer needs a library at home. Moreover, he is constantly on the move. He negotiates at meetings and collects information at congresses. He contracts for commissions with publishers. The latter now determine along with him which books must be written.[65]

By the 1980s, the enormous increase in empirical research activity antici-pated by Heidegger and described by Bernard Forscher in his brick-making analogy was being translated into very real changes in the roles and aspira-tions of academics. An extensive survey across the USA of attitudes and practices in all spheres of higher education led Ernest Boyer to echo Heidegger's words with the observation that 'basic research has come to be viewed as the first and most essential form of scholarly activity, with other functions flowing from it'.[66] Boyer contrasted this 'restricted view of scholarship'[67] with the traditional view of 'a variety of creative work carried on in a variety of places, and its integrity was measured by the ability to think, communicate and learn'.[68] In the intervening years since Boyer described 'basic research' as having become the dominant form of schol-arly activity, a *Gestalt* switch between foreground and background has occurred to the extent that scholarly activity is usually now regarded as a (rather lowly) form of research. For example, the definition provided for the Research Excellence Framework (REF), which has had a huge influ-ence on academic planning and strategizing in the UK, subsumes scholarship under the broader remit of research, and defines it as 'the creation, development and maintenance of the intellectual infrastructure of subjects and disciplines, in forms such as dictionaries, scholarly editions, catalogues and contributions to major research databases'.[69] This shift confirms the view expressed earlier that the primary activity of university academics, at least in the UK, is no longer scholarship but research. Thus, in response to the REF definition, some UK universities are offering a 'scholarship' career pathway for those academics who are not meeting the research publication requirements of a 'full' lectureship.[70] As Andreson points out, the terms 'research' and 'scholarship' have for some time been used to distinguish between the people who really do the research and the rest who merely need to keep up with it.[71]

As we might expect of a definition that is intended primarily as a way of operationalizing and measuring research 'quality', the REF definition of scholarship relates it to specific types of published outputs, and as such it would appear that the majority of university academics would probably engage in little or no scholarship during their entire career. Furthermore, by narrowing down what counts as scholarly output to contributions to diction-aries, catalogues and databases, scholarship has *by definition* been more or less removed from our scholarly journals. For the purposes of the REF, then, scholarship is a subset of research, and not even a very important or valuable one. Seen in this way, the job of the scholar is to follow behind researchers, tidying up their loose ends, summarizing their findings into catalogues and databases, and acting as general housekeepers to the 'intellectual infrastructure'. In the space of 50 years, we have gone from a situation where scholarship was so foundational to academic life that it was simply taken for granted, to one where the eminent UK educationalist Ronald Barnett is able to pose, without any hint of irony, the question: 'Can scholarship be taken seriously in the contemporary university, or do the contemporary discourses and ideologies of the university squeeze it out?'.[72]

The university in ruins

Since Readings charted the demise of north-American higher education in the early 1990s, the development of the corporate University of Excellence has spread and intensified. I have attempted in this chapter to argue that both the teaching and research agendas of the post-historical university have, in recent years, become distorted by the need to participate and compete in a global financial market. This has led to a shift from *culture* to *excellence* as the validating principle or (to employ the predominant corporate language) the 'mission statement' of the university; from *truth and emancipation* to *efficiency and profitability* as the 'big stories' or grand narratives that the university tells in order to justify and pursue its mission; and from researcher and teacher *accountability* to *administration and accountancy* as the means of maintenance and evaluation of the effectiveness of the mission.

For Readings, this turn to the corporate values and practices of the business world has, as the title of his book suggests, left the university in ruins. Whilst he spends the majority of his book detailing the nature of the decline of the university, the final two chapters are devoted to how we might 'dwell in the ruins' in a way that involves neither 'militant radicalism' nor 'cynical despair'. Unfortunately, Readings was tragically killed in an air crash in 1994 as he was making the final revisions to his book, leaving his wife and colleague Diane Elam to 'complete the revisions on which Bill was working, taking his notes and our many conversations as my guide'.[73] Readings' prescription for dwelling in the ruins of the university is thus somewhat brief and sketchy, and we can perhaps only guess at where his thinking and writing would have led him.

In the remainder of this book I intend to use some of Readings' ideas and speculations as a starting point, a blueprint, for how those of us who are not content with the demands made upon us by the post-historical University of Excellence might create a space where a community of scholars 'could think the notion of community otherwise...where the impossibility of such models can be thought'.[74] This can be seen as an appeal for a space within the ruins for radical self-critique in which 'to make the destruction of existing cultural forms by the encroachment of the open market into an opportunity for Thought rather than as an occasion for denunciation or mourning'.[75] The aim of this book, then, is not to denounce or to mourn the passing of the modern Enlightenment university, but to suggest ways in which the resources of the University of Excellence, which has come to replace it, can be subverted to provide an opportunity for thought.

Chapter 2

Thinking as a subversive activity

'Men fear thought more than they fear anything else on earth – more than ruin, more even than death. Thought is subversive and revolutionary, destructive and terrible; thought is merciless to privilege, established instructions, and comfortable habits; thought is anarchic and lawless, indifferent to authority, careless of the well-tried wisdom of the ages.'

Bertrand Russell, *Principles of Social Reconstruction*, 1916

Dwelling in the ruins

Bill Readings' thesis, which he outlined in his book *The University in Ruins*, is that the modern idea of the Enlightenment university has been superseded by the University of Excellence, in which efficiency and profitability are no longer means but are ends in themselves, and where administration has become the route to those ends. The traditional idea of the university as a place where culture is the *raison d'être,* and where truth and emancipation are the goals, lies in ruins. The question, then, is this:

> At the twilight of modernity, which is also the twilight of the University as we have known it, can another way be found to think in the University? This is to ask whether the University, once stripped of its cultural mission, can be something other than a bureaucratic arm of the unipolar capitalist system.[1]

As academics, it would appear that we have three options: we embrace the corporate ethos of the University of Excellence; we adopt a stance of 'militant radicalism' in overtly resisting that ethos; or we choose to dwell in the ruins of what the University of Excellence has destroyed. Readings rejects the first option as unacceptable and the second as untenable. It is impossible to adopt an authentically radical stance in the corporate University of Excellence because radicalism can be packaged and sold as a commodity just as readily as intellectualism or sporting prowess. The 'radical university' will be attractive to a certain type of student and academic, and the ethos of the University of Excellence is that radicalism is a saleable commodity, so long as it is *excellent* radicalism.[2] For Readings, then, the ruins of the Modern University cannot be restored to their former glory; there can be no return, no project of rebuilding the edifices of the Enlightenment that does not stem either from romantic nostalgia or cynical despair.

In the penultimate chapter of his book, Readings begins to sketch out a plan for how we might 'dwell in those ruins without recourse to romantic nostalgia'.[3] We must not, he says, follow the Romantics by regarding the ruins of the Enlightenment university *as ruins*, that is as a symbol of some lost unity of thought from a bygone golden age that stands alongside present-day structures, reminding us of 'the claim for knowledge as an inter-active encounter with tradition'.[4] Rather, we must simply accept and negotiate among the ruins: this is where we find ourselves and this is where we must continue to live and work. Thus, 'to inhabit the ruins of the University must be to practice an institutional pragmatism'.[5] Such pragma-tism entails a recognition that the university is no longer required to make transcendental claims for its justification and function, that it no longer plays an ideological role in the development of 'good' or 'productive' citizens, nor in the production of the culture that binds those citizens to the nation-state.

The university with no idea

The Enlightenment ideals of truth and emancipation can no longer be sustained in this post-historical, postmodern world, and the idea of the university as intimately attached to the cultural project of the nation-state is no longer tenable. The university has lost its external referents, which have been replaced in the post-historical university by the empty idea of excel-lence, an idea that cannot serve as a referent since it does not refer to anything in particular. In semiological terms, it is an 'empty signifier', a sign without a referent. However, Readings claims that there can be no turning back, no romantic search for new referents, new grand narratives of legiti-mation for the university. Instead, 'we should try to think what it may mean to have a university that has no idea, that does not derive its name from an etymological confusion of unity and universality'.[6]

Readings claims that 'this suggestion comes at the very beginning of what must be for me a long process of thinking',[7] and one which, tragically, he did not have time to complete. However, we know that his long process of think-ing began with the proposition that the empty idea of excellence be replaced with 'the empty name of Thought'.[8] He explains that:

> I say 'name' and I capitalise 'Thought' not in order to indicate a mysti-cal transcendence but in order to avoid the confusion of the referent with any one signification. The name of Thought precisely is a name in that it *has no intrinsic meaning.*[9]

Whilst it might appear on first sight that Readings is merely replacing one empty signifier with another, he points out that 'Thought, unlike excellence, does not masquerade as an idea'.[10] Whereas the idea of excellence is attractive precisely because no one feels the need to ask what it means, Thought *demands* to be problematized: 'Thought does not function as an answer but as a *question*'.[11] By regarding Thought as a name rather than as an idea, we raise the question of what it is that Thought names, and this question must be kept permanently open in order to prevent the name of Thought from slipping back into an idea, 'from founding a mystical ideology of truth'.[12] By regarding Thought as a name rather than as an idea or concept, Readings is making the point that Thought is *self-consciously* empty and without signification. Thought is *what happens* when we think, and to paraphrase Roland Barthes, 'to think' is an intransitive verb, a verb with no object.[13] The whole point of Thought, then, lies in keeping open the question of what Thought names, that is, the question of what it *really means* to think and hence the question of what the university with no idea is *for*.

Whereas the Enlightenment university was concerned with the preservation and dissemination of culture, and the University of Excellence aims for the smooth administration of students and research projects through the bureaucratic system, Readings' university with no idea proposes a return to the notion of *Thought* as the primary purpose of the university. This, of course, is not to suggest that the corporate University of Excellence has completely abolished thinking in favour of administration, nor that the production of thought and the production of money are mutually exclusive activities. However, we should be careful not to confuse the *idea* of thought with the *name* of Thought, nor the purpose and product of thinking with the act of thinking. The purpose of thinking in the University of Excellence is largely as a means to an end, whether it is the end of writing a research bid or a new curriculum. To that extent, thought is more or less the unwanted by-product of thinking. Furthermore, because thinking in the University of Excellence is directed towards an agreed, tangible and predetermined end, the resulting thought[14] of the various individual thinkers is largely in agreement, and where it is not, consensus is sought. As the university comes to resemble more and more a large business corporation, so thinking is becoming more and more corporate and convergent. In contrast, the name of Thought, as we have seen, functions as a question rather than an answer; the purpose of thinking in the university with no idea is not to achieve consensus, but rather to *avoid* consensus by keeping open the question of Thought. Thinking in Readings' university with no idea has no end, except for more thinking.

Thought, accountability and radical critique

The refusal of Thought to seek consensus applies also to the reflexive question: *What is Thought?* Readings suggests that this amounts to 'the question of how the university is to be evaluated', which demands 'a philosophical separation of the notions of *accountability* and *accounting*'.[15] The question of Thought is therefore the question of academic accountability rather than corporate accountancy; it is a *calling to account* that extends to the very foundations of the academy. Thought demands that we interrogate (or, to use corporate language, that we *audit*) the traditional ways of thinking that predominate in the university, and is therefore a reflexive practice (a praxis) that turns back on itself. Put another way, Thought suggests *a particular kind of critique* that looks inwards at itself rather than outwards at the world; a critique that, as Michel Foucault observes:

> is not [merely] a matter of saying that things are not right as they are, it is a matter of pointing out on what kinds of assumptions, what kinds of familiar, unchallenged, unconsidered modes of thought the practices that we accept rest.[16]

Thought is not concerned with making judgements that 'things are not right as they are', but with laying bare and calling into question the fundamental assumptions upon which those 'things' are founded. In this sense, Thought might be described as *radical*, as a questioning of the very roots (from the Latin *radix*) of the academy.

The (re)establishment of the importance of Thought in the university is no easy matter. On the one hand, the University of Excellence is a bureaucratic organization geared to making money, in which every activity is tied to a funding stream and a tangible outcome, and where there is no place for reflexive thinking that produces nothing but more Thought. Readings recognizes this problem, pointing out that 'nothing in the nature of the institution [of the University of Excellence] will enshrine Thought or protect it from economic imperatives'.[17] Clearly, the university with no idea cannot appeal to the new grand narratives of economy and efficiency, since:

> Thought is non-productive labor, and hence does not show up on balance sheets except as waste. The question posed to the University is thus not how to turn the institution into a haven for Thought but how to think in an institution whose development tends to make thought more and more difficult, less and less necessary.[18]

On the other hand, Thought entails a radical critique that calls into question the very foundations on which the University of Excellence has been built. The business organization that is the University of Excellence cannot be expected to tolerate such a radical practice as Thought, which is not only unproductive but also undermines the very ethos of productivity.[19] The rehabilitation of Thought cannot realistically be achieved by creating a new type of institution or even by reforming the existing one. The challenge is rather to find a way of pragmatically 'dwelling in the ruins' of an institution that makes Thought more and more difficult and less and less necessary, without resorting to a bizarre and anachronistic return to the now-dead traditional Enlightenment university. Meeting this challenge, of course, can only be a subversive activity; a resistance and rejection from within of the 'quality' mission, of the grand narratives of efficiency and profitability, and of administration and accountancy (and of administrators and accountants) as their guarantors. The restoration of Thought therefore entails a 'calling to account' of the university that demands accountability rather than accountancy.

This calling to account has traditionally fallen to the discipline of philosophy, which Kant[20] originally positioned at the very heart of the Modern University, to the extent that the idea of a university without a philosophy department has been (and for some still is) almost literally unthinkable. For Readings, as we have seen, the project of the university has until recently been tied to that of national culture, and the ousting of the discipline of philosophy from its central role in the Modern University can be seen as the consequence of a deep-seated shift away from philosophy in favour of 'national literature' at the root of our cultural identity.[21] More recently, the so-called 'postmodern age' has witnessed the fragmentation of the concept of national culture and with it the rise of cultural studies, which, as Readings points out, can only come into existence as an academic discipline at the point at which culture ceases to have any unifying or even referential function in society and the university.

My analysis of these shifts rests on the understanding that the generation and dissemination of knowledge and power are intimately linked, and that epistemological and political changes within the university proceed in unison. Foucault fused them into a single power/knowledge plexus, and his use of the term 'discipline' to describe fields of academic endeavour betrays the (hidden) desire within the academy to police the internal and external boundaries of the university and to punish those who attempt to transgress them.[22]

I will firstly examine Readings' account of the demise of the academic discipline of philosophy and the subsequent rise of 'national literature' and latterly cultural studies at the heart of the life of the university. I will then argue that this *disciplinary* shift has been accompanied by a parallel *political* shift from accountability to accountancy, resulting in the ousting of radical critique from its central role of calling the Modern University to account. I will finally suggest that the practice of Thought can be restored through the rehabilitation of the philosopher back into the daily life of the university.

After philosophy

As Readings observes, Kant identifies philosophy as the discipline or 'faculty' that united all other faculties within the early Modern University through the imposition of reason. For Kant, philosophy is unique amongst the faculties insofar as it has no content; it is, rather, the free exercise of rational inquiry, and, as such, the foundation of the principle of academic freedom.[23] As Readings points out, 'each discipline seeks . . . what is essential to it. And what is essential to philosophy is nothing other than this search for the essential itself: *the faculty of critique*.'[24] As academic philosophy became more and more distanced from everyday life and culture during the course of the twentieth century,[25] public understanding and focus of culture shifted from the philosophical to the literary.[26] Thus, as Readings observes, there has been a move 'from philosophy to literary studies as the major discipline entrusted by the nation-state with the task of reflecting on cultural identity'.[27] Readings suggests that this shift in the centre of gravity of the university was detectable from as early as the mid-nineteenth century, for example in the work of John Henry Newman in the UK and Friedrich Schlegel in Germany. For Schlegel, literature was more rooted in national culture and identity and less elitist than philosophy, and thus better suited to promote 'the whole intellectual existence of a nation'.[28] Similarly, although Newman associates 'intellectual culture' with philosophy, Readings points out that Newman is not referring to philosophy in a disciplinary sense but rather as 'a habit, a personal possession, and an inward endowment'.[29] When it comes to identifying the academic discipline charged with maintaining and disseminating national culture, Newman echoes Schlegel in his view that 'by great [literary] authors the many are drawn up into a unity, national character is fixed, a people speaks . . .'.[30]

Eighty years later, C.P. Snow identified the 'two cultures' dominant in academic life as the scientific and the literary, and failed even to mention the existence of philosophy. The reason for Snow's omission could be simply an acknowledgement of the traditional Kantian role of the discipline of philosophy as standing outside of the two cultures and attempting to mediate between them. However, the thrust of Snow's argument is that the discipline of literature was beginning to appropriate this traditional role of intellectual culture-carrier. Thus, he recalls:

> I remember [the mathematician] G.H. Hardy once remarking to me in mild puzzlement, sometime in the 1930s: 'Have you noticed how the word "intellectual" is used nowadays? There seems to be a new definition which certainly doesn't include Rutherford or Eddington or Dirac, or Adrian or me. It does seem rather odd, don't y'know.'[31]

Snow's 'Two Cultures' adversary F.R. Leavis reinforced this idea that the centre of gravity of the university had shifted to the discipline of English Literature when he wrote, at the end of the 1960s, that

> a centre of consciousness for the community must have its centre in an English school . . . a focus of cultural continuity can only be in English . . .

There is no other access to anything approaching a full continuity of mind, spirit and sensibility.[32]

Since the 1990s, economic and market imperatives have seen a subsequent shift away from the discipline of literature towards what we might refer to as 'the Studies'. With a growing emphasis within the University of Excellence on training for employment, the so-called 'pure' disciplines such as literature, chemistry and sociology (to take just three examples) are being replaced by subjects related to occupations rather than to academic disciplines. These subjects, many of which have previously had little or no presence in the university, are being 'academicized' (that is, redefined as disciplines) by the attachment of the word 'studies'. Thus, we have in recent years witnessed the arrival and growth within the university of new disciplines such as 'business studies', 'tourism studies', 'nursing studies', 'sports studies' and so on. Under this regime, disciplines such as literature and sociology, which are falling out of favour with students because of a lack of perceived application to the world of work, can be reinvigorated under the rubric of 'literary studies' and 'social studies'. For Readings, the paradigm case of 'the Studies' is the discipline of cultural studies, which has emerged 'as the strongest disciplinary model in the humanities in the Anglo-American University'.[33] We can see, then, a gradual falling away of the influence of philosophy over the past 150 years as market forces begin to dictate the agenda of the University of Excellence.

Wittgenstein and the demise of philosophy

I have suggested above that the demise of philosophy as the discipline central to the academic life of the university has been accompanied by a parallel shift in the way that the university regulates and accounts for itself. As the discipline of literature became established as the protagonist of the historical project of national culture in the modern university, philosophical critique made way for literary criticism as the mode by which the university looked critically at itself, that is as the mode through which the university *thought*.

Jürgen Habermas traces the demise of philosophy as the home of Thought in the academy to its growing association with science and the scientific method that began in the late nineteenth century with the rise of positivism. Habermas's thesis is that philosophy gradually moved from a reflective and transcendent theory of universal knowledge to a 'pseudo-normative regulation of established research'. Philosophy therefore brought about its own downfall through an exclusive association with a scientific method 'emptied of philosophical thought'. Thus, 'philosophy's position ... has been undermined by the movement of philosophical thought itself. Philosophy was dislodged from this position by philosophy.'[34]

This 'movement of philosophical thought' can be seen most clearly in the work of Ludwig Wittgenstein, arguably the most influential philosopher of the twentieth century. Wittgenstein's early reputation was founded on a single short work, the *Tractatus Logico-Philosophicus*, first published in 1921, which became one of the most prominent texts of the Vienna Circle of logical positivism. This work presented the so-called 'picture theory' of language, which posited a strong logical and grammatical relationship between propositions and facts, and suggested that 'Propositions cannot represent logical form ... Propositions *show* the logical form of reality. They display it.'[35] For Wittgenstein, the traditional role of philosophy is, therefore, literally meaningless or nonsensical, since it has largely confined itself to raising metaphysical questions and expressing propositions that 'arise from our failure to understand the logic of our language'.[36] This critique, of course, applies also to the *Tractatus* itself. Thus:

> My propositions serve as elucidations in the following way: anyone who understands me eventually recognizes them as nonsensical, when he has used them – as steps – to climb up beyond them. (He must, so to speak, throw away the ladder after he has climbed up it.) He must transcend these propositions, and then he will see the world aright.[37]

Philosophy is therefore presented by Wittgenstein in the *Tractatus* as a meta-science or meta-language and the *Tractatus* as merely a tool to be discarded once it has been used to climb above the restrictions of everyday philosophical and scientific propositions. He concluded the *Tractatus* with the well-known aphorism or proposition that 'What we cannot speak about we must pass over in silence.'[38]

This somewhat curious demand that philosophy should burn its bridges or kick away the ladder behind it, attempts (if I may be permitted to mix my metaphors even further) to both eat the cake and have it. On the one hand, Wittgenstein aligns himself strongly to scientific empiricism, whilst on the other hand philosophy is presented as the discipline that transcends science. Thus, natural science is the totality of all true propositions, and philosophy is not one of the natural sciences, but rather 'The word "philosophy" must mean something whose place is above or below the natural sciences, not beside them.'[39]

Although it was critical of the traditional role of philosophy, the *Tractatus*, in itself, should not be regarded as bringing about the demise of philosophy as the academic heart and soul of the university. On the contrary, Wittgenstein's position can be seen as neo-Kantian insofar as he sought to re-establish philosophy as a meta-science, the discipline that looks down upon and regulates what can and cannot be expressed in the form of scientific propositions; as the discipline that decides what knowledge and which disciplines do and do not belong in the university.

Following the publication of the *Tractatus*, Wittgenstein abandoned philosophy for several years, believing that he had uttered the final word on the subject. He returned to Cambridge in 1929 and later worked as a hospital porter and laboratory assistant during the Second World War (although he was Austrian, he found himself a citizen of Germany following the *Anschluss* of 1938). During this period, Wittgenstein embarked on his final philosophical project, which sought to revise and largely refute his earlier views on language and its role in philosophy. Published in 1953, two years after his death, *Philosophical Investigations* challenged Wittgenstein's earlier assertion that the problems of philosophy could be determined and solved through logical and linguistic analysis. Instead, he argued that words do not refer simply to the external world, but rather take their meaning from the ways that they are used in everyday speech. Thus, he points out:

> We are so much accustomed to communication through language, in conversation, that it looks to us as if the whole point of communication lay in this: someone else grasps the sense of my words – which is something mental: he as it were takes it into his own mind.[40]

But language is *not* simply the transmission of ideas between minds, and at this point Wittgenstein introduces the idea of 'language games' as a means of showing how the same word or sentence can take on a variety of meanings depending on the 'game' that the speaker and listener are 'playing'. For example, the words 'the student has passed the course' can be stated as a piece of information in response to a request (denotative language game). However, if the same words are uttered by the chair of an examination board, they perform the symbolic role of actually passing the student (performative language game). Language is therefore not a transparent medium through which meaning is simply and clearly transmitted from speaker to listener, but rather a series of games relating to different 'forms of life', each with its own set of rules, in which we engage with one another.[41] Communication between people does not depend so much on a shared understanding of the meaning of words as on a shared agreement about the rules of the game in which they are being used. For Wittgenstein, most disputes about meaning can be shown to arise from misunderstandings about the contexts and games in which words are being used. The role of philosophy is therefore not to settle disputes according to some meta-scientific or meta-academic overview, but rather to demonstrate that the seeming dispute over meaning can be reduced to a dispute over the use of words.[42] As Wittgenstein claims, the aim is not to *solve* problems but to *dissolve* them. Philosophy, then, is not so much an academic discipline as an activity or a particular mode of thinking that we can apply in order to resolve academic disputes.

Barthes and nouvelle critique

Wittgenstein's later philosophy shared a number of similarities with the work of the Swiss linguist Ferdinand de Saussure, who is credited as the founder of both semiotics and structuralism.[43] His theory that words do not have an intrinsic meaning but take their meaning from their relationships with other words prefigured Wittgenstein's injunction 'Let the use of words teach you their meaning'[44] by 40 years and laid the foundation for Roland Barthes's structural (and later post-structural) approach to literary criticism, allowing him to blur the boundaries between philosophy and literature, and hence to begin the process of establishing literature as the 'new philosophy'.[45]

We can, perhaps, narrow down the moment at which literature made its first serious bid to be the discipline through which the university looked critically at itself to 1963, when Barthes published a collection of three essays entitled *Sur Racine*,[46] followed by a further collection, *Essais critiques*,[47] which attempted to justify the critical stance taken in the earlier essays. Barthes distinguishes between traditional or 'university criticism' on the one hand, and *nouvelle critique* on the other. Whereas traditional criticism attempts to understand a literary work solely in relation to the mores and conventions of 'good literature', Barthes's *nouvelle critique* looks beyond the context of the work and, indeed, beyond the discipline of literature. In retrospect, we can see in Barthes's manifesto an attempt by the discipline to look outward towards its wider role in the academy rather than restricting itself only to the world of literature.[48]

Raymond Picard, Professor of Literature at the Sorbonne, responded to Barthes's critique of the work of Racine with a paper entitled *Nouvelle critique ou nouvelle imposture*,[49] provoking a response from Barthes that addressed the broader principles of the nature and function of criticism and its role in the academy.[50] In particular, Barthes argued that if literary criticism was to function more widely *as critique*, then it must transcend its traditional role in literature of merely passing judgement:

> So long as criticism had the traditional function of judging, it could not but be conformist, that is to say in conformity with the interests of the judges. However, the true 'criticism' of institutions and languages does not consist in 'judging' them, but in *perceiving*, in *separating*, in *dividing*. To be subversive, the critic does not have to judge, it is enough that he talks of language instead of using it.[51]

To be subversive was, for Barthes, to critique the language games or basic assumptions of the institution within which one operates. In this short extract, then, we can see in a nutshell the shift from the discipline of literature as being concerned solely with literary texts to it taking on a universal significance within the academy as a whole. As Barthes points out, 'what new criticism is reproached with today is not so much that it is "new", but that it is fully "criticism"'.[52]

Barthes's response to Picard focused on rebutting what he termed 'critical verisimilitude' or 'criticism for the masses'. Verisimilitude refers to a particular taste in literature 'deposited in the mind of men by tradition, Wise Men, the majority, current opinion, etc.',[53] which Barthes elsewhere terms the *doxa* or accepted opinion. Thus, critical verisimilitude involves judgements that concur with and support the *doxa*, and 'what is convincing in a work or discourse is that which contradicts none of these authorities'.[54] Furthermore, this verisimilitude or *doxa* is rarely stated explicitly; it is 'that which *goes without saying*';[55] we are generally only aware of the *doxa* when we run up against its limits.

The problem for Barthes was that if literature was to become the new 'master discipline' of the academy, then literary critique must extend beyond simply reinforcing the academic *status quo*. However, we can see that the function of traditional university critique was primarily to police the existing boundaries of academic discourse and to pass judgement on any writers or academics who challenged the *doxa* of accepted academic opinion. For Barthes, these judgements stemmed from 'a habitual process of confused logic' by which

> The unbelievable proceeds from the forbidden, that is to say from the dangerous: disagreements become divergences, divergences become errors, errors become sins, sins become illnesses, illnesses become monstrosities.[56]

In this way, any opinion or critique that poses a threat to the *doxa* is demonized and thereby suppressed. This 'confused logic' can be seen most clearly in certain religious doctrines, where to contradict 'that which goes without saying' is forbidden and dangerous (even to *say* 'that which goes without saying' is dangerous because it immediately calls it into question). Disagreements with the *doxa* are therefore presented as divergences from the true path, and any divergence from the *doxa* is, by definition, *paradoxical* and therefore an error. A mere glance at the history of religious persecution will quickly show how disagreements are presented as sins, illnesses and/or monstrosities and are punished accordingly, depending on the times and the culture.

Although the 'confused logic' of old critique typically 'goes without saying' and therefore passes largely unnoticed in the academy, some of the more extreme (and thus more dangerous) critics of the *doxa* have evoked overt and sometimes ruthless responses. For example, Friedrich Nietzsche has perhaps threatened the *doxa* more than any other academic writer of the past 200 years, provoking an extreme response from the historian Felipe Fernandez-Armesto:

> Like Hitler, Nietzsche hated people but loved animals. He died defend-
> ing an abused horse. His prescription for the world was a morbid fantasy,
> warped and mangled out of his own lonely, sickly self-hatred, a twisted
> vision from the edge of insanity.[57]

Such is the economy of language here that Fernandez-Armesto manages to
implicate Nietzsche in sins, illnesses and monstrosities in just one short
paragraph.

A similar approach of damning by association can be seen in various other
attempts to discredit those (often continental) writers who challenge the
doxa. Thus, Roger Scruton lines up 'humane educated Englishmen' such as
'Coleridge, Ruskin, Arnold and – in the political sphere – Macaulay,
Gladstone and Disraeli' against European intellectuals, whom he describes as
'a synthesis of French bohemianism and Russian nihilism' and who, 'as we
know from the cases of Marx, Lenin, Mao, Sartre, Pol Pot and a thousand
more, are dangerous'.[58] As Barthes would no doubt have pointed out, this is
a poor and cynical substitute for academic discourse, and whilst traditional
university critique might generally masquerade as objective academic criticism, when push comes to shove it reveals its covert policing role.

We can see, then, that Barthes's challenge to the academic *doxa* is not only
epistemological but also political. In extending his criticism of traditional
critique beyond the field of literature, he implicates *all* disciplines, including
philosophy, in supporting and maintaining the *doxa*. By offering a new set of
criteria with which the academy as a whole might look critically at itself and
its practices, he sought to displace the traditional role of philosophy at the
intellectual heart of the university by attempting to subvert the existing
'philosophical' rules established by the ancient Greeks and adhered to 'without raising questions of method' ever since.

Unsurprisingly, this project met with strong opposition from those in the
academy who had most to lose from such a challenge, not least from the
discipline of philosophy. Since the 1920s, English- and German-speaking
philosophy had been dominated by the school of logical positivism and
latterly by the analytic philosophy that developed from logical positivism,
which sought to place philosophy on an empirical footing alongside science.[59]
When faced with the challenge from post-structuralist literary critique, the
analytic philosophers dealt with it by firstly redefining it as a branch of philosophy and then rejecting it as not rigorous enough to meet the rigid and
exacting criteria they had imposed on the discipline, most notably that of
verificationism.[60] This strategy can be seen, for example, in the open letter
written by Barry Smith and signed by 20 analytic philosophers against a
proposal by Cambridge University to award an honorary degree to Jacques
Derrida. Smith and colleagues objected to the award on the grounds that
Derrida's work 'does not meet accepted standards of clarity and rigour', that
he had stretched 'the normal forms of academic scholarship beyond

recognition' in a series of 'attacks upon the values of reason, truth and scholarship', and that he was not, after all, a philosopher.[61]

The threat posed to the *doxa* by Barthes and those (mostly French-speak-
ing) post-structuralists who followed him was taken seriously enough for
Barry Smith to follow up his open letter with the accusation that:

> Many current developments in American academic life – multicultural-
> ism, 'political correctness', the growth of critical theory, rhetoric and
> hermeneutics, the crisis of scholarship in the humanities departments –
> have been closely associated with, and indeed inspired by, the work of
> European philosophers such as Foucault, Derrida, Lyotard and others.[62]

Although Smith and his colleagues were unsuccessful in blocking the award
of an honorary doctorate to Derrida, post-structuralist literary critique
continued to come under sustained attack not only from the discipline of
philosophy, but also from the sciences'[63] and was rapidly losing its recently
won place as the site of Thought in the university.

The rise of cultural studies

As the role of maintaining and disseminating national culture finally moved
beyond the remit of the academy, the discipline of literature was replaced by
'cultural studies' as the new critical voice of the University of Excellence. It
might seem somewhat odd that cultural studies should take on such a role
just at the moment when the idea of the University was becoming divorced
from the project of national culture, but as Readings points out:

> It seems to me that the idea of Cultural Studies arises at the point when
> the notion of culture ceases to mean anything vital for the University as
> a whole. The human sciences can do what they like with culture, can do
> Cultural Studies, because culture no longer matters as an *idea* for the
> institution.[64]

Readings' point, then, is that cultural studies could *only* come to prominence
as a discipline once culture ceased to be the unifying project of the university.

For Readings, the rise of cultural studies originates in a desperate move by
those academics whose disciplines have been 'closed down' (both figuratively
and literally) as a consequence of the market agenda of the corporate
University of Excellence. As he points out, the discipline of cultural studies
arises 'out of the predicament of those who are excluded from within, who
can neither stay nor leave'.[65] It is a radical response to the ruination of the
university that demands that it must be abolished; that the ruins of the
Enlightenment project must be cleared before something new might be
built. However, we have already seen that this is not Readings' solution to

the problem of the University of Excellence, and he adds that such an undertaking is counter-productive at best and downright cynical at worst. Thus, 'the cry of cultural studies that the University must be left behind has proved a particularly fruitful way of staying in the University'.[66] Furthermore, although culture no longer matters as an overarching 'regulatory ideal for research and teaching',[67] the discipline of cultural studies continues to promote itself as 'a hegemonic institutional project',[68] albeit a hegemony with no epistemological grounding and with no attempt to consider the place of Thought in the University.

For Readings, this empty (we might say Thoughtless) demand for the overthrow of the university amounts to 'throwing out the baby and keeping the bathwater',[69] and we could therefore argue that the project of cultural studies is *authoritarian* rather than *authoritative*. Thus, 'Cultural Studies presents a vision of culture that is appropriate for the age of excellence'[70] and the idea of radical internal critique of the institution of the university itself was finally abandoned with the rise of the University of Excellence during the 1990s. The attempt by literary critics to reintroduce Thought by radicalizing university critique had largely failed. Thirty years after Barthes's manifesto for *nouvelle critique*, Terry Eagleton noted that the repressive nature and function of traditional critique had changed little, and that academic critique remained 'typically conservative and corrective, revising and adjusting particular phenomena to its implacable model of discourse'.[71]

A community of dissensus

The failure of the discipline of literature to offer a sustained reflexive institutional critique has left the university bereft of any critical regulating function and has allowed the administrators and bureaucrats to bring about its corporatization, and hence its ruination, in the name of excellence and efficiency. At the same time, the vacuum left by the abdication of cultural studies as the 'master discipline' has opened up a space for philosophy to regain its traditional Kantian role of calling the university to account. However, the time of philosophy as a meta-discipline whose role is to regulate all other disciplines is long past. As Wittgenstein concluded, the role of philosophy is not to *solve* intellectual problems nor to *resolve* academic disputes, but rather to *dissolve* issues through an examination of language games. Thus, as well as triggering the demise of philosophy as an authoritative discipline with something concrete and substantive to say about the world, Wittgenstein's *Philosophical Investigations* also laid the foundations for the possibility of a resurgence of philosophy as a way of reintroducing Readings' proposed 'name of Thought' into the university.

Whilst this philosophical (re)turn to Thought might be seen as a return to the ethos of the Enlightenment, Readings is not suggesting a nostalgic rebuilding of the ruined university; he is not advocating a unified thinking machine or even a 'think tank' of minds all attuned to the quest for a solution to a shared problem, but rather a practice of 'thinking together' without a preordained or desired outcome. Readings' injunction to 'Think together' is, in fact, a radical departure from the Enlightenment mission of unity and universality, and has the aim *not* of achieving consensus but *dissensus*; not convergence of thought and ideas but *difference*. Thinking together is therefore thinking in parallel, thinking alongside one another with no pressure to reach agreement; indeed, the purpose of thinking together is precisely to *avoid* coming to agreement.

Readings' proposed 'University with no idea', where the purpose of thinking together is to open up a space for more thinking and where the production of Thought replaces the generation of money as the primary aim of teaching and research, does not and cannot exist independently from the existing institution. As Readings suggests, those who wish to subvert the corporate mission of the University of Excellence must continue to dwell among the ruins 'pragmatically'. Change, he claims, 'comes neither from within nor from without, but from the difficult space – neither inside nor outside – where one is'.[72] He continues: 'To say that we cannot redeem or rebuild the University is not to argue for powerlessness; it is to insist that academics must work without alibis, which is what the best of them have tended to do.'[73] That is to say, we must not use the continuing decline of the university as an excuse for withdrawal from the academy; we must do what we can from the position we find ourselves in and with the resources at our disposal.

The university with no idea is therefore a university within the University, populated by teachers, researchers and students thinking alongside one another in dissensus. In place of the traditional Enlightenment *uni*versity, signifying as it did a unity of thought and a unification of ideas, we might strive to create what I will refer to as a *Para*versity, which runs unseen or unnoticed alongside, and in parallel with, the University of Excellence, and in which Thought proceeds along parallel lines and with no pressure to converge as 'big ideas'. I have coined the term '*para*versity' not only to denote a parallel enterprise, but also to stand in contrast to a *uni*versity which, as Readings pointed out, suggests a project of unity and universality.[74] The Enlightenment university, then, was concerned with a convergence of thought towards a single unified and universal truth, whilst the University of Excellence seeks a single currency, a saleable commodity of knowledge and information in which there is no room for doubt or dissent. In each case, the aim of the university is universal consensus. In contrast, the paraversity is concerned not with convergence on a single unified and universal truth, but with parallel lines of thought that never meet, regardless of how far they are pursued. As we have seen, Readings refers to this antithesis of consensus as *dissensus*, the pursuit of difference. Thinking together in the paraversity is thinking in dissensus. The purpose of thinking together is not to arrive at agreement, not to resolve or shut down discussion and debate, but to keep it open and alive.

The paraversity, then, might function as an invisible, subversive, virtual institution that exists *alongside* the visible University of Excellence, neither inside it nor outside it. Indeed, it would be misleading to locate the paraversity in space just as it is a mistake, say, to locate the postmodern in time. The paraversity is nothing more nor less than a *radical critique* of the University of Excellence in the same way that postmodernism is a radical critique of modernism.[75] Indeed, we might go further and suggest that the paraversity is the project of rehabilitating radical critique in the name of Thought and restoring it to its rightful place at the heart (or perhaps the soul) of the university. To borrow Gilbert Ryle's phrase, we might regard the paraversity as the ghost in the University of Excellence machine. More prosaically, the function of the paraversity is to call the University of Excellence to account; to instigate and operate full intellectual accountability alongside existing corporate accountancy.

It is apposite at this point to return to the question posed by Readings at the beginning of this chapter: 'At the twilight of modernity, which is also the twilight of the University as we have known it, can another way be found to think in the University?'[76] I have suggested that the project of radicalizing the university from within in the name of *nouvelle critique* has largely failed, and the call to abolish the University of Excellence has been revealed as merely another way of maintaining and progressing it. Readings' final word on how we might dwell in the ruins in a productive and constructive way is that we must form a 'community of dissensus',[77] and he remained hopeful that such a community had the potential to exist amidst the ruins of the Modern University. I have proposed the notion of the paraversity as the virtual space where such dissensus might occur. The question left largely unanswered by Readings, and to which my attention must now turn, is how, and on what foundations, the paraversity might be built.

Part 2

Building the paraversity

'Only someone who carries the idea of the university in himself can think and act appropriately on behalf of the university.'

Karl Jaspers, *The Idea of the University*, 1923

Part 1 of this book provided a brief exposition of Readings' thesis of the ruined university. It ended with some thoughts about how we might, in his words, 'dwell in the ruins' without recourse to militant radicalism or cynical despair, and issued a challenge for those of us who are dismayed and dissatisfied by what the university has become to construct a new 'virtual space', a paraversity, alongside the corporate 'ruined' university. In Part 2, I will attempt to think about how Readings might have developed his ideas further had he lived, beginning with some thoughts about what he meant by his curious injunction to dwell in the ruins of the university.

Ronald Barnett, writing shortly after Readings' death, concludes that 'Readings has it half right. The university *is* a ruined institution, but we do not have to dwell in its ruins'.[1] I will suggest in Chapter 3 that it is Barnett who is half right in failing to think sufficiently about what Readings might have been implying in his use of the words 'ruin' and 'dwell'. My intention is to show that Readings is most certainly not precluding the construction of a 'new university' in his injunction to dwell in the ruins of the old one. As he astutely points out, 'the University as an institution is now up for grabs',[2] and he had no qualms about grabbing it. In thinking about how we might build something new amongst the ruins of the old, I turn in Chapter 3 to the work of Heidegger on the nature of dwelling and Deleuze on rhizomatic structures. If Heidegger is the building contractor for the paraversity, Deleuze is the architect. Chapter 4 develops further the idea of the paraversity as a critical community of thought and attempts a subversive reading of the mission statement of my own university in order to demonstrate that its apparent scholarly goals conceal a corporate commercial enterprise. Chapter 5 brings Part 2 to a close with some suggestions for a new values-based way of being in the university based on Michael Oakeshott's ideal of 'knowing how to behave in a certain way and trying to behave in that way'. I explore and develop Oakeshott's injunction by proposing the values of being good, being collegiate and being radical, under the rubric of a 'fourth mission' for the paraversity and with the intention of reinstating Readings' idea of the 'name of Thought' back where it belongs as the beating heart of the university.

Chapter 3

The philosophy of dissensus

'And yet philosophy cannot give up, lest idiocy triumph in actualized unreason.'
Theodor Adorno, *Negative Dialectics*, 1966

Imagining the paraversity

If, as Readings tells us, the institution of the university is in ruins, then the questions to which we must now address ourselves concern what might be built in its place and how we might continue to function with integrity in a climate where Thought is considered, at best, an unnecessary luxury, and at worst to be undermining the corporate mission to generate and sell information.

At the end of the previous chapter, I proposed the idea of the paraversity as an invisible, subversive, virtual institution that exists *alongside* the visible University of Excellence, neither inside it nor outside it. I suggested that it would be misleading to locate the paraversity in space, which begs the question of what it might mean to build or construct it. Readings offers little specific advice about how such an institution might be built or what it might look like, although he does provide us with a number of hints and clues about its salient features. Firstly, his proposed solution to the problem of the ruined university involves neither clearing away the ruins nor attempting to rebuild them, but simply 'to dwell in those ruins without recourse to romantic nostalgia'.[1] This entails viewing the ruins pragmatically and without regarding them as the remains of some bygone golden age, as, for example, the Victorians venerated the ruins of Ancient Greece. Secondly, we should dwell 'without alibis'; that is, in good faith and from a proactive position of strength. As Readings points out, this is where we find ourselves and we have to construct a way of doing something meaningful from within the ruins without excuses and 'without offering ourselves up for tourism'.[2] Thirdly, in the absence of a physical edifice, we must construct what Readings refers to as a 'community of dissensus', a community of critical thinkers in which Thought proceeds along parallel lines with no pressure to converge or conform. And fourthly, of course, we must continue to satisfy the demands of our employers in the University of Excellence whilst at the same time subverting its corporate aims and working practices.

Dwelling in the ruins

Readings repeats several times the injunction that we should *dwell* in the *ruins* of the Enlightenment university, which suggests that he chose his words carefully and deliberately. The image of the ruin has been a recurring metaphor throughout the period of the Enlightenment, offering 'a way to phrase our own relation to the past'.[3] As Brewer points out:

> Ruins fascinate, and we can begin to historicize this fascination in the eighteenth century by locating in the scientific excavations at Herculaneum and Pompeii that began around mid century.[4]

On the one hand, he claims that the ruin represents 'the sense on the part of modern consciousness of an acute separation and alienation from the past'.[5] On the other hand, however, it is a separation that can be bridged through the application of reason, science and technology. The ruin, then, 'represents the remnants of the past as concealed yet accessible to those who have the techniques – tools and knowledge – to unearth and understand them'.[6] Ultimately, however, Brewer regards the project of modernity as gradually to subsume the ruin, to bury it, so that each ruin becomes the foundation for a subsequent new structure. Thus:

> In transforming the past into the luminous sign of a rational, progressive history, the past disappears as such, pillaged in the name of progress rather than preserved.[7]

Significantly, this modernist transformation of the ruin is not the approach advocated by Readings who, as we have seen, urges us to dwell in the ruins without either restoring them to their Enlightenment glory or else using them as the foundation for some new, modern, post-Enlightenment structure. Readings' injunction to *dwell* in the ruins can therefore be read as a rejection of the modernist urge to clear away the past in order to create a new and better future.

But whilst the ruin is a well-established Enlightenment trope, Readings' use of the metaphor of dwelling is, at first sight, somewhat more unusual and even archaic. The English verb 'to dwell' generally signifies inertia, passivity and a continuation of the *status quo*, and it is hard to believe that this passive acceptance is what Readings is suggesting when he urges dissatisfied and disaffected academics to dwell in the ruined university. As he points out, to say that we cannot redeem or rebuild the university is not to argue for powerlessness, but rather to offer an active challenge to the corporate ethos of the

University of Excellence. On the face of it, then, his choice of the verb 'to dwell' rather than a more active verb such as 'to work' or 'to build' is somewhat curious, and requires further thought and exploration.

A clue to Readings' intended meaning might be found in Martin Heidegger's lecture *Building Dwelling Thinking*,[8] a text with which Readings would almost certainly have been familiar. In this lecture, given in 1951 in honour of the German composer Conradin Kreutzer, Heidegger seeks to redefine the temporal relationship between building and dwelling, and ultimately between dwelling and thinking. He begins with the traditional common-sense view that first we build, and, having built, we are then able to dwell in our buildings. He suggests, however, that this understanding of the German verb *wohnen* (to dwell), by which 'we attain dwelling, so it seems, only by means of building',[9] is mistaken. Drawing on the etymology of the word *bauen* (to build), Heidegger demonstrates that *wohnen* and *bauen* have essentially similar meanings. He concludes that 'building is really dwelling' and 'building as dwelling unfolds into the building that cultivates growing things and the building that erects buildings'.[10] Heidegger thus effectively reverses the temporal relationship by suggesting that first we dwell in the sense of growing and cultivating, what Heidegger refers to as 'settling', and only once we have settled do we erect buildings: 'we do not dwell because we have built, but we build and have built because we dwell, that is, because we are *dwellers*';[11] and '*only if we are capable of dwelling, only then can we build*'.[12]

In the final paragraphs of his text, Heidegger associates dwelling with thinking, a connection that appears also in the English language in the sense of dwelling on a thought or an idea. To dwell is to ponder or to reflect, which again should not be taken in a passive sense. To *dwell* on a point or on an argument is gently, but thoroughly, to explore or probe, to examine it from all sides. In contrast, to *build* an argument is to construct a case from a particular point of view with a specific end in mind. This distinction between building and dwelling as ways of thinking is developed further in a later lecture from 1955, where Heidegger asserts that 'there are, then, two kinds of thinking, each justified and needed in its own way: calculative thinking and meditative thinking'.[13] Heidegger echoes Readings' argument that Thought is no longer valued in the university (indeed, that Thought is unproductive and is therefore actively to be discouraged) in his statement that 'man today is in *flight from thinking*',[14] and warns that 'calculative thinking may someday come to be accepted and practiced *as the only* way of thinking'.[15] Heidegger is not suggesting that we no longer think, but that we no longer value thinking as a reflexive activity or as an end in itself. Thus, thought is more and more directed towards specific goals and purposes:

> Calculative thinking computes. It computes ever new, ever more promising and at the same time more economical possibilities. Calculative

thinking races from one prospect to the next. Calculative thinking never stops, never collects itself. Calculative thinking is not meditative thinking, not thinking which contemplates the meaning which reigns in everything that is.[16]

Meditative thinking, which Heidegger also refers to as in-dwelling (*Inständichkeit*), stands in contrast to calculative thought and shares many of the characteristics that Readings would later attribute to what he calls 'the empty name of Thought',[17] that is of thinking as a form of reflexive and radical critique. Thus, meditative thinking has no end other than an openness to further thought, and it encourages us 'not to cling one-sidedly to a single idea, nor to run down a one-track course of ideas',[18] but rather to open up multiple lines of inquiry that do not seek convergence on a single solution. Meditative thinking, in common with Readings' 'empty name of Thought', is speculative, critical and largely non-productive.[19]

If we accept that Readings had been influenced by Heidegger's notions of *building as dwelling* as a way of being in the world and of meditative *in-dwelling* as an alternative to calculative thinking, then to dwell in the ruins is not merely to exist passively and aimlessly in what remains of the Enlightenment university, but rather to settle and to stake a claim on the contested academic territory that Readings considers to be currently 'up for grabs'.[20] Ultimately, to dwell in the ruins of the university is to make our home in it, to cultivate it and thus to build on it. However, building-as-dwelling does not necessarily entail the modernist notion of building-as-erecting: 'Building in the sense of preserving and nurturing is not making anything.'[21] To dwell in the ruins of the university is to build in a particular kind of way. It does not require the physical construction of bricks-and-mortar buildings but rather the building of a community that values a certain kind of thinking, what Readings call a 'community of dissensus'.[22]

Building a community of Thought

Readings observes that 'the University of Culture is grounded in the notion of communicative transparency'.[23] In contrast to this Enlightenment ideal of the straightforward and unproblematic transmission and dissemination of thoughts and ideas between individual scholars, between professors and students and between academic disciplines, the construction of the paraversity requires the nurturing of a particular kind of community of thought that is bound together *not* by the Enlightenment desire for resolution and consensus through clear and transparent communication, but by a commitment to what Readings refers to as 'dissensus', the shared desire to avoid closing down argument and debate through compromise and concession.[24] A community of dissensus is one 'that has relinquished the regulatory ideal of communicational transparency, which has abandoned the notion of identity or unity';[25] that is to say, a community united only by the desire not to present a united front. It is not a community of consent, but neither is it a community of *dissent* in any negative sense of the word. It is a community united neither by a common 'yes' nor by a common 'no'.[26] If it is resisting or rejecting the University of Excellence, it is doing so with a diversity of ideas and in a plurality of voices.

If such a community of Thought is to become a reality, it cannot subscribe to the modernist notions of commonality and inclusivity, but must equally resist the view that the opposite of inclusion is exclusion. Readings offers the idea of the community of dissensus as 'the political as an instance of community' and as 'a sharing that does not establish an autonomous collective subject who is authorised to say "we" and to terrorize those who do not, or cannot, speak in that "we"'.[27] It is a community that presupposes nothing in common, but which is built on a series of social bonds and obligations that Readings suggests are neither knowable nor redeemable. That is to say, we[28] cannot identify and articulate the forces of obligation that hold such a community together, and neither can we cash them in. The community of dissensus, which I am proposing as the defining feature and structural foundation of the paraversity, is therefore constituted by those members of the University of Excellence who, for a variety of reasons, refuse to speak with one corporate voice, who refuse to say 'we' in the collective sense but who subscribe to a plurality of singularities.[29] Readings insists that such a community would be dedicated neither to 'the project of full self-understanding (autonomy)' nor to a 'consensus as to the nature of its unity', but instead 'would seek to make its heteronomy, its differences, more complex'.[30]

At first sight, it might appear that the notion of a plurality of singularities is at best no more than a loose grouping of individual persons with little or nothing to unite them apart from a reflexive concern with their own incompatabilities, and at worst an oxymoron. In order for the paraversity to exist in a substantive and proactive sense as something more than a coalition of the unwilling or a disunity of no-sayers, it requires lines of communication and an organizing structure. The corporate University of Excellence, like almost all capitalist organizations, has adopted a structure that best facilitates the flow of power and authority from top to bottom or from centre to periphery. Such structures, which Deleuze and Guattari refer to as arborescent, resemble trees in their organizing principles. Thus, 'Arborescent systems are hierarchical systems with centres of significance and subjectification.'[31] Managerial structures in organizations of this type are usually displayed hierarchically in tree-like diagrams, and power flows unidirectionally from the roots, via a central trunk, to the outermost branches and twigs.

An arborescent structure is clearly inappropriate for a community that refuses to say 'we'; a community that resists any attempt at centralized control, hierarchical organization and executive action. Deleuze and Guattari address this challenge of how to conceptualize, conceive and establish a plurality of singularities by introducing the principle of 'multiplicity', which 'is reducible neither to the One nor the multiple'[32] and which adopts the structure of the rhizome. 'Rhizome' is a botanical term for an underground stem system that spreads horizontally by sending out roots and shoots from its nodes. As Deleuze and Guattari explain:

> A rhizome as subterranean stem is absolutely different from roots and radicles. Bulbs and tubers are rhizomes . . . any point of a rhizome can be connected to anything other, and must be. This is very different from the tree or root, which plots a point, fixes an order.[33]

Rhizomatic structures are not planned out in advance and purposively constructed. Rhizomes grow organically and largely unnoticed; we need only dig in order to uncover the network of *ad hoc* and multiple connections and patterns of communication already in place.

Organizing the paraversity rhizomatically not only obviates the need for formal managerial structures such as faculties and departments, but also cuts across the traditional intellectual organization of the university into academic disciplines. Thinking together is not constrained by disciplinary boundaries, but it would be equally misleading to conceptualize it as cross-disciplinary, multidisciplinary or even interdisciplinary. Rather, thinking together calls the very notion of disciplinarity into question. Readings proposes 'an abandonment of disciplinary groundings' but not at the expense of 'a simply amorphous interdisciplinary space'.[34] The organization and structuring of knowledge is essential to ordered and coherent thinking, and Readings proposes 'a shifting disciplinary structure'[35] as thinkers come together temporarily in order to pursue specific short-term collaborative teaching and research projects.

We might therefore imagine the paraversity as an underground, acentred, non-hierarchical, trans-disciplinary network of singularities, any and all of whom might have unmediated and unrestricted access to any and all of the others. The Paraversity-as-rhizome has no clear boundaries and no straightforward defining criteria. As Deleuze and Guattari point out, the injunction of rhizomatic organizations is not *to be* but rather *to connect*, to establish subterranean links and alliances:

> A rhizome has no beginning or end; it is always in the middle, between things, interbeing, *intermezzo*. The tree is filiation, but the rhizome is alliance, uniquely alliance. The tree imposes the verb 'to be', but the fabric of the rhizome is the conjunction, 'and . . . and . . . and . . . '.[36]

To those working outside of it, the paraversity would be all but invisible. It would have no formal membership, no command structure, no recognizable academic disciplines, no departments or departmental heads, in fact no overt outward signs of its existence. To those within it, the paraversity would offer encouragement to think and to work differently, 'to move between things, establish a logic of the AND, overthrow ontology, do away with foundations, nullify endings and beginnings'.[37] In short, the paraversity would offer an opportunity to participate in a community of dissensus; an opportunity for Thought with no pressure to conform to, or converge on, a unified or universal consensus.

It is becoming ever more difficult to take such a non-aligned and non-consensual stance in the corporate university in which all are expected, if not compelled, to display the university brand, to sign up to the university mission statement, and to meet the university performance indicators. These obligations cannot completely be circumvented, and the establishment of the paraversity is therefore neither an invitation nor an excuse to opt out of the University of Excellence. As Readings insists, we must attempt to dwell in the ruins 'pragmatically' as best we can, without recourse to alibis. Rather than an outright and overt rejection of the trappings, values and goals of the corporate University of Excellence, we must, each in our own individual way, subvert them. The community of dissensus that is the paraversity must therefore operate alongside (or perhaps beneath) and parallel to the corporate and consensual University of Excellence without ever touching or being touched by it.

Thinking rhizomatically

The image and form of the rhizome offers a way of envisaging a structure for the paraversity that allows it to grow and flourish unseen and uncontaminated by the arborescent command structure of the corporate University of Excellence. More importantly, however, the rhizome provides a model (or, as Deleuze and Guattari would suggest, a map) for how the community of dissensus that is the paraversity might *think*. Whereas an arborescent community is concerned with ordered and rigorous (that is, rigid) thought, with academic discipline(s), with focus and consensus, a rhizomatic community of dissensus fosters horizontal links between disparate thinkers and disparate thoughts that cut across traditional academic disciplines and subjects, and which resist categorization and resolution. Whereas arborescent thought has an ontological mission to determine and define what *is* the case, rhizomatic thought is a conjunctive alliance to establish the logic of the AND. Whereas the aim of arborescent thought is to pare away alternative discourses in order to arrive at consensus, rhizomatic thought attempts to open up new discourses, to keep debate open for as long as possible, to resist the idea of the final word. Whereas arborescent thought is concerned with discrete projects, with beginnings and endings, with means and ends, rhizomatic thought works with processes rather than outcomes; that is, only with middles. But as

Deleuze and Guattari tell us, the middle is not a compromise, it is not (an) average: 'the middle is where things pick up speed'.[38]

There is a danger that a rhizomatic community of Thought of this kind might expand into nothing more than an accumulation of individual thinkers thinking individual thoughts more or less in isolation and with no organizing shape or purpose. If the project of rhizomatic thought is conjunctive rather than ontological, then the rhizome that is the paraversity might simply inflate and extend itself in all directions like a balloon filling with hot air with little or no reference to what Readings calls *the name of Thought*, that is with Thought as the process of calling the university to account through critique. Rhizomatic thought should not be seen as eschewing logic or organizing principles; it is just that its logic is different from arborescent logic. It is not the linear analytic logic of the tree, but the integrative and *Gestalt* logic of the map. For Deleuze and Guattari, 'all of tree logic is a logic of tracing and reproduction'. Arborescent thought, thought that is based on the logic of the tracing, is disciplinary; it restricts as it organizes; it traces clear linear paths of authority and accountability; it determines what thought, what methods, what subject matter is permitted within a given discipline and what belongs rightly to other disciplines. Arborescent thought polices the boundaries and disciplines transgressions. In contrast:

> The rhizome is altogether different, a *map and not a tracing* ... What distinguishes the map from the tracing is that it is entirely oriented towards an experimentation in contact with the real. The map does not reproduce an unconscious closed in upon itself; it constructs the unconscious. It fosters connections between fields, the removal of blockages ... The map is open and connectable in all of its dimensions; it is detachable, reversible, susceptible to constant modification. It can be torn, reversed, adapted to any kind of mounting, reworked by an individual, group or social formation.[39]

A map does not tell you where you are or in which direction you should proceed. You need to know already where you are in order to make use of a map, and it can be used to travel in any and all directions. Maps demand an interaction with the world, a constant interplay between the depiction and reality, 'an experimentation in contact with the real'. Maps might depict borders and boundaries, but they also reveal routes and pathways across those borders.

Rhizomatic thought (that is, Readings' 'name of Thought') maps out the boundaries between disciplines whilst at the same time inviting their transgression. Rhizomatic thought is concerned with *how* the university thinks rather than *what* the university thinks. Rhizomatic thought does not locate itself in any particular discipline or faculty and its form and content is not subject to the incessant reordering and restructuring of disciplinary boundaries. Rather, as we have seen, the paraversity-as-rhizome calls into question *the very idea* of organized and enduring disciplines. Rhizomatic thought is a response to Readings' call for a return to thinking, that is to the idea of philosophy as 'the purely autonomous moment when knowledge reflects upon itself'.[40]

The (re)turn to philosophy

This latest turn to reflexive thinking is, at least on the face of it, a return to the Kantian notion of a faculty within the university whose essence is the quest for reason and critical (self-) analysis. However, Kant recognized that the exercise of critique required a certain political independence not generally afforded in his time to university faculties. Thus:

> It is absolutely essential that the learned community at the university also contain a faculty that is independent of the government's command with regard to its teachings; one that, having no commands to give, is free to evaluate everything, and concerns itself with the interests of the sciences, that is, with truth; one in which reason is authorised to speak out publicly.[41]

Kant entrusted this evaluative and regulatory task to philosophy,[42] but in order to enact such a role, the faculty of philosophy had to be free of government control.

Although universities are no longer subject to state regulation in quite the way that they were in Kant's time, the principle still holds: philosophy is defined as the exercise of pure reason,[43] and reason is, in turn, defined as the power to judge freely and autonomously 'according to the principles of thought in general'.[44] The faculty of philosophy must therefore stand outside of the usual regulatory mechanism of the university, which in the corporate University of Excellence means outside the requirement to account for itself according to the empty idea of 'excellence', which is usually defined in terms of economic criteria such as the acquisition of research grants and student fees. Such a position is nowadays untenable, and it is for this reason, as well as because of the ideological shifts in the role and function of the university discussed in the previous chapter, that the discipline of philosophy first lost its position as the regulating faculty of the university and is now losing its presence completely. The idea of a university without a department of philosophy is no longer the unthinkable prospect that it was even 50 years ago, to the extent that my own university, along with many others in the UK and elsewhere, closed its philosophy department some years ago with very little fuss or complaint from the wider academic community.

Clearly there is no scope for the return of 'pure' philosophy to the university as 'the faculty of critique';[45] as a faculty without portfolio and with little visible means of external financial support. However, to claim that philosophy has no place in the corporate university in the disciplinary sense is not to say that there are no longer any *philosophers* in the university. As Readings points out, the closure of philosophy departments resulted in teaching and research staff from these departments 'spinning off into applied fields in which experts provide answers rather than refining questions – medical ethics being the most obvious example'.[46] These applied philosophers perform the same role as any other academic in the corporate university: they seek academic consensus and provide answers to specific disciplinary questions rather than conforming to Kant's ideal of the 'pure' philosopher 'who is not an artificer in the field of reason, but himself *the lawgiver of human reason*'.[47] Philosophy, to the extent that it still exists as a discipline, has signed up to the corporate mission of the University of Excellence and now performs the function of answering questions rather than formulating them.

The differend

However, a return to philosophy in the Kantian sense might be achieved in ways that do not entail the establishment of a new faculty or department. Kant's notion of the philosopher as lawgiver is taken up in a distinctly post-Kantian (we might even say 'postmodern' way) by Jean-François Lyotard in his book *The Differend*, which opens with the bold statement that 'The time has come to philosophize'.[48] As I suggested in the previous chapter, this call is not simply a demand for a return to some golden age of certainty imposed through meta-narratives, but rather an acknowledgement that those times have past. Lyotard sets his call to philosophize in the context, first, of the 'linguistic turn' of western philosophy, and second, of 'the decline of universalist discourses'.[49] To philosophize in this sense, then, is to agree 'not to be done with "language"'[50] that is, to accept with Wittgenstein that the role of philosophy is to explore and expose the linguistic roots of academic and political disputes rather than to settle them through the imposition of a philosophical meta-language. The focus of philosophy is therefore on language games, or what Lyotard now terms 'phrase regimens'. He continues: 'there are a number of phrase regimens: reasoning, knowing, describing, recounting, questioning, showing, ordering, etc. Phrases from heterogeneous regimens cannot be translated from one into the other.'[51] That is to say, disputes in which the protagonists are employing different language games or phrase regimens can only be resolved through the medium of one or other of the phrase regimens in which their arguments are couched (or through a third), and, in either case, such a resolution will favour the party in whose phrase regimen the judgement is made.

Lyotard refers to such disputes, where the two sides are expressing their arguments in terms of incompatible phrases, as *differends*, which he distinguishes from 'litigations', which are disputes couched within a common phrase regimen and which therefore *can* be settled equitably and without prejudice to either party. Lyotard explains what is at stake at the very beginning of his book:

> As distinguished from a litigation, a differend [*différend*] would be a case of conflict, between (at least) two parties, that cannot be equitably resolved for lack of a rule of judgement applicable to both arguments. One side's legitimacy does not imply the other's lack of legitimacy. However, applying a single rule of judgement to both in order to settle their differend as though it were merely a litigation would wrong (at least) one of them (and both of them if neither side admits this rule) . . . A wrong results from the fact that the rules of the genre of discourse by which one judges are not those of the judged genre or genres of discourse.[52]

Readings draws on a legal example to illustrate the difference between a litigation and a differend.[53] There is a general consensus in the developed world regarding land rights, and disputes about the ownership of particular areas of land can therefore usually be settled in court by a judge with reference to the law. Assuming that all parties are in agreement about the validity and application of the legal framework, such disputes would count as litigations. In order to give an example of a differend, Readings relates the plot of Werner Herzog's film *Where Green Ants Dream*, in which Australian aboriginals come into conflict with a mining company that claims ownership of some land sacred to the aboriginals:

> The mining company has one kind of claim ('legal title', deeds, etc.). The aborigines have another kind of claim (sacred buried objects). There is not simply a dispute as to who owns the land; the notion of 'property' as such is the locus of a differend.[54]

When asked to present the sacred objects as 'evidence', the aboriginals reply that they cannot, since to look upon the sacred objects would be a sin, resulting in the death of the viewer. As Readings points out, 'No tribunal can resolve the case, either way, without victimizing one side or the other'.[55]

In the context of the academy, litigations can be said to occur in cases of disagreement within the parameters of a particular paradigm, discourse or methodology. For example, academic disputes over the carbon dating of an archaeological find or about the meaning of a passage from a literary text are cases of litigation that can usually be settled from within the parameters of the discourse in which the dispute arose. In contrast, disputes about the validity of carbon dating or about whether there can ever be a single authorial meaning of a work of literature are essentially disputes about different understandings or interpretations of the discipline as a whole, or else about what count as valid methodologies for scholarship within those disciplines. These disputes cannot be settled by reference to an agreed rule or convention and can therefore be regarded as differends. On rare occasions, differends can occur between, as well as within, disciplines. The example from Chapter 1, where Raymond Tallis attempted to judge the scholarly worth of the humanities according to the evidence-based criterion of medicine, generates such a differend, since there is no rule or principle for making judgements about scholarship in the humanities that would satisfy both parties. Whatever the judgement, at least one side would feel wronged or, at best, misunderstood.

Towards a philosophy of dissensus

The traditional Enlightenment university (and, more recently, the post-historical University of Excellence) has organized its faculties and disciplines in ways that are designed to avoid the creation of differends. As Readings points out:

> It is a community whose dialogue is about nothing, in the sense that no issues for dispute are engaged. There are no differends, no radical and incommensurable differences, only arguments as to the exact nature of what it is that we agree on.[56]

When differends *are* encountered, the usual approach is to attempt to resolve them in order to arrive at an authoritative and (Lyotard would contend) an authoritarian solution, in either the quest for transcendental or universal truth or the pursuit of commerce. Lyotard refers to those academics who facilitate this consensual process as 'intellectuals' and contrasts them with 'philosophers'. Thus the intellectual attempts to impose a single grand narrative on the academy, whether it is truth, emancipation or, more recently, excellence: 'An intellectual is someone who helps forget differends, by advocating a given genre . . . for the sake of political hegemony.'[57]

In contrast, the role of Lyotard's philosopher is threefold. Firstly, the philosopher is called upon to 'bear witness' to differends; that is to promote and encourage cases of conflict that cannot be resolved; to keep debate open by refusing to advocate a given genre for the sake, as Lyotard puts it, of political hegemony. Secondly, it is the task of the philosopher to interject in disputes where a differend is being treated as a litigation; that is where a dispute between two incommensurate phrase regimens is being settled according to the rules of one or other (or neither) of them. In these cases, the philosopher is called upon to find, as Lyotard puts it, the 'impossible idiom' for phrasing them, or else to provide an 'enigmatic judgement', a judgement without rules,[58] that is a judgement that does not arise from the application of one or other phrase regimen. Thirdly, the philosopher recognizes that the genre of philosophy is subject to its own strictures; that there is no genre whose hegemony over the others would be just. The philosophical genre, which looks like a metalanguage, is not itself (a genre in quest of its rules) unless it knows there is no metalanguage.[59]

The genre of philosophy is therefore no different from any other genre, except insofar as it recognizes itself as such. As 'a genre in quest of its own rules', a genre that acknowledges its own contingency, it is able to make unique 'enigmatic' judgements appropriate to the individual demands of the unique situation.

The (re)turn to philosophy therefore requires no new departments, no building programmes, no management structure. 'Philosophy' no longer names a faculty or even an academic discipline; 'philosophy', in the sense in which it is being used here, refers to a language game, a genre of discourse or a mode of thinking. 'Philosophy' is the attempt to maintain differends, to keep Thought alive, to promote dissensus, to refuse to have the last word. We might even say that 'philosophy' is our manner of dwelling in the ruins of the Enlightenment university. The paraversity, then, is a subversive community of philosophers in which 'thought takes place beside thought'[60] in an attempt to resist the turn to corporatism and to call the self-styled University of Excellence to account. It is a community in which each individual thinker is able to 'plug in' to any and all others, regardless of disciplinary and hierarchical boundaries; and it is subversive in the sense that each individual thinker has to be seen to be satisfying the demands of the corporate mission of the University of Excellence whilst at the same time attempting to undermine and subvert them through the reinstatement of reflexive critique and non-productive Thought. The question of how we might dwell subversively in the corporate University of Excellence is the subject of the next two chapters.

Chapter 4

Being subversive

'The subversion of established institutions is merely one consequence of the previous subversion of established opinions.'

John Stuart Mill, *A Few Observations on the French Revolution*, 1857

Subversion and the paraversity

We now arrive finally at the crux of the matter, which Readings was surely positioning himself to address before his untimely death in 1994: How can we open up a space where we might think together in an institution that values only commerce and administration? There are, of course, many ways of responding to this question. Some writers have called for a return to Enlightenment values whilst others demand a radical review or even the overthrow of the institution of the university. Readings' argument, and mine, is that neither is feasible nor even desirable. Readings suggests that we must find ways to dwell in the ruins of the Enlightenment university 'pragmatically' and 'without alibis', and I have attempted to flesh out some of his sketches for how to do this into a vision for the paraversity as a subversive community of dissensus.

It is important at this point to understand what is involved and what is at stake in being subversive. Despite the commonly held understanding of the verb 'to subvert' as to overthrow or to destroy, its Latin roots suggest an undermining or a change of direction or influence from below. Thus I am not arguing for the overthrow of the corporate university; the call to subversion is not revolutionary in the sense of bringing down the system; it is not, as Readings puts it, a cynical demand for the abolition of the university as a way of defining and maintaining our place in it. It is neither a way of erecting nor of demolishing, but simply of dwelling. Subversion can only effectively be carried out from within; it is the attempt to bend the current structures and mechanisms of the university to breaking point, but no further. The aim of the paraversity, insofar as it has one, is not to work against the corporate mission (which would, in any case, be untenable) but to work in parallel to it by subverting its purpose and adding value(s) to its product;

that is to say, to reintroduce the 'non-productive labor of thought' alongside the production and sale of information. As academics in the paid employment of the corporate University of Excellence, we are contractually obliged to publish papers and to produce graduates, but we have the added, parallel obligation to do so in ways that pay attention to *quality*, as well as quantity and to human *values* as well as financial value. As Readings tells us, the practice of Thought differs from the corporate pursuit of excellence 'in that [Thought] does not bracket the question of value'.[1]

We saw in the previous chapters that, for Roland Barthes, to be subversive is to undermine the dominant discourse or *doxa* through a radical critique of its language games, terminology and syntax. Derrida, borrowing from Heidegger, refers to such critique as *deconstruction*, the meticulous pulling apart of texts from within. Despite attempts by American literary theorists to develop deconstruction as a method of textual analysis, Derrida insists that 'deconstruction doesn't consist in a set of theorems, axioms, tools, rules, techniques, methods... There is no deconstruction, deconstruction has no specific object.'[2] That is to say, deconstruction does not impose from the outside (in any case, Derrida insists that there is no outside: '*il n'y a pas de hors-texte*'[3]); texts naturally and spontaneously deconstruct themselves. A deconstructive reading of a text subverts its intended meaning, its message, by drawing attention to the contradictions and challenges to that message implicitly and (sometimes) explicitly already there. Deconstruction simply reads the text against itself, thereby not only subverting its *meaning* but, more fundamentally, subverting the *very idea* of a unitary and univocal text that is able to communicate a clear and unambiguous message. Deconstruction, then, teases out the multiple meanings that coexist in all texts, often tucked away in the margins, and plays them one against the other.

Subverting the mission

The *doxa* of the corporate university is displayed in its simplest and most overt form in the public statement of its mission, which reveals not only its aims and objectives but also its underpinning aspirations and basic assumptions. If, as John Stuart Mill suggests, the subversion of established institutions is a consequence of the previous subversion of established opinions,[4] then the most effective place to begin to undermine the institution of the university is with a deconstructive critique of its opinions in the form of its mission statement.

Stefan Collini has described the university mission statement as 'a kind of cross between an extended dictionary definition of the term "university" and an advertising brochure for an upmarket health club'.[5] Although the wording of the text might vary, once we begin to examine the subtext, most university mission statements tend to express more or less the same aims, objectives, aspirations and assumptions. Thus Readings wrote of 'banal and cliché-ridden mission statements (which are all the same from university to university)'[6] and which 'all claim that theirs is a unique educational institution.' They 'all go on to describe this uniqueness in exactly the same way'.[7] One possible reason for this conformity is perhaps because, as William Melody observes, 'the primary measure of the modern university is simply to do what its funders want it to do'.[8] To deconstruct one mission statement is thus to deconstruct them all. I therefore propose to examine the mission statement of my own university in what follows, not because it is in any way special, but precisely because it is not. It is neither one of the top 'Russell Group' research-intensive institutions, nor one of the former polytechnics that were awarded university status in the UK during the 1990s, some of which might continue to regard their primary mission as teaching rather than research. It is, quite simply, an average university that considers being 'research-led' as the defining factor of excellence. A second reason for focusing on my own university is that I believe that critique, like charity, should begin at home.[9]

The mission statement of my university is divided into the typical three sections of research, education and service, each of which appears at first sight to be grounded in Enlightenment values, but all of which, on closer inspection, can be seen as responses to the corporate agenda of the University of Excellence. Indeed, the very act of dividing the aim and purpose of the university into a series of discrete 'missions' can be seen as a production-line strategy of division of labour through the separation of roles and functions in the pursuit of efficiency and maximized output. The overall vision of my university, as stated in its *Strategic Plan*, is to position itself as 'a strong research-led university that could support wealth-creating activity and be a major driver for economic regeneration . . .'.[10] Certain conclusions can immediately be drawn from a vision that contains the words 'research', 'wealth' and 'economic', but not 'education', 'students' or 'culture'. This, clearly, is not an Enlightenment vision in the classic sense of the university as home to culture and learning, but a response to external drivers where finance is both the measure and the reward of success, and research is the primary means by which it is achieved.

The mission of research

Unsurprisingly, then, the first part of the mission states that my university *will provide an environment of research excellence, with research being undertaken that is world-leading and internationally recognised and that informs all other activities at the University.* This carefully (if somewhat clumsily) worded sentence might appear on first sight to be a statement of scholarly intent, but a closer reading reveals that it is not so much expressing the Enlightenment commitment to scholarship by *doing* research as the corporate commitment to administration by '*providing an environment* of research excellence'. It is not altogether clear what an environment of research excellence might look like, nor what might be involved in providing one, but that is perhaps the point. As we saw in Chapter 1, Readings considers the word 'excellence' to be an empty signifier that can be applied to justify *any* aim or mission. Just as an award for excellent parking can be given for attempts either to restrict or to increase the number of cars on campus, so 'research excellence' can mean whatever the university wishes it to mean. In this case, we can discern its intended meaning by what follows: the mission statement of my university suggests that an environment of research excellence should lead to research that is 'world-leading and internationally recognised'.

The subtext of the mission only fully reveals itself once we are aware that the somewhat vague and amorphous terms 'world-leading' and 'internationally recognized' are quoted directly from the UK Research Excellence Framework (REF) assessment exercise, which is used by the government to allocate research funding. Since the criteria used in the REF for measuring 'world-leading' and 'internationally recognized' research are widely perceived to be large research grants from prestigious funding bodies and publications in 'high-impact' research journals, it might reasonably be concluded that the mission of my university is to provide an environment that facilitates the writing of funding bids and research reports. This, as I have argued, is a corporate administrative endeavour rather than an academic or scholarly one. This part of the mission statement ends with a commitment that research will 'inform all other activities at the University', thereby reinforcing the intention that the university will be 'research-led'.

The mission of education

The second part of the mission statement of my university promises that it *will deliver an outstanding student experience, with teaching of the highest quality that produces graduates equipped for distinguished personal and professional achievement.* As before, what might on first sight look like an expression of scholarly intent is, on closer inspection, a corporate commitment to consumer satisfaction where, somewhat confusingly, the student is both the customer *and* the product. This is ostensibly a statement of the educational part of the mission, and yet the word 'education' is nowhere mentioned.[11] I have already suggested that the concept of education is problematic to the corporate university, which values only tangible and measurable outputs. I have also suggested that many students no longer come to university in order to be educated, nor even to acquire new knowledge, but only to obtain a degree certificate that can then be cashed in for a good salary in order to repay their student loans and debts. In other words, the role of the corporate university is not to educate but, as the mission explicitly states, to produce graduates.

It is therefore hardly surprising that the term 'education' has been falling out of favour in the university for some years, to be replaced by 'learning and teaching'. Although this term is often used as a direct replacement for 'education', it seems to me that something has been lost, and that delivering opportunities for learning and teaching amounts to something significantly less than providing an education. The precise nature of what is lost when a university replaces a scholarly commitment to education with the commercial aims of *producing* graduates and *delivering* teaching is open to debate. In a political and economic climate where quality has been redefined as quantity and where universities are required to justify their existence in terms of measurable outcomes, it is increasingly difficult to present a convincing argument for education. Whereas the 'quality' of learning can be measured by student performance in examinations, and the 'quality' of teaching can be assessed and rated through student evaluation forms, education cannot so easily be quantified, and therefore, from the corporate perspective, it has no tangible existence.

The mission statement of my university goes a step further than many others in omitting not only all references to education, but also to learning, which is replaced by the term 'student experience'. Once again, this shift in the language through which the university describes its mission reflects a wider corporate agenda of customer relations. Universities in the UK are judged, rated and compared on their teaching using statistical data gathered through the National Student Survey (NSS), which is administered by a well-known market research agency, and by various other internal and external measures of student satisfaction. These findings have enabled my own university to proclaim in all seriousness that 'the ability of staff to communicate effectively' is 91 per cent, and 'the enthusiasm of staff' is 85 per cent.[12] Whether this means that 85 per cent of staff are enthusiastic, that the average rate of enthusiasm of staff is 85 per cent of some ideal maximum level of enthusiasm, or whether the statistic has some other meaning, is not made clear.[13]

Whilst students' involvement and participation in their education is an important and laudable aim, the inflated importance placed on the results of student satisfaction surveys has shifted the focus of the educational mission of the university away from student learning towards 'student life-cycle interaction' and 'student-facing functions'.[14] The dangers of assessment-driven learning, where students are only concerned with learning to pass course assignments, are well known. However, we are now starting to witness a new phenomenon of assessment-driven teaching, where the most important 'educational' outcome for lecturers is not the facilitation of learning, but rather to obtain a high score in the NSS by ensuring that their students are 'satisfied'.

The mission of service

The third and final part of the mission of my university states that *The University Community will be a powerhouse for growth in the regional economy, and will greatly enrich the community and cultural life of Wales. It will contribute to the health, leisure and well-being of citizens in South West Wales and beyond.* This so-called 'Third Mission' of the university has been the subject of perhaps the greatest corporate reworking and reconceptualization over the past 200 years. We have seen that the fundamental purpose, the 'first mission', of the nineteenth-century Enlightenment university was neither teaching nor research, but rather serving the community through the maintenance, production and dissemination of national culture. John Henry Newman, writing in the mid-nineteenth century, speculated on the relative importance of the educational and cultural missions of the university:

> I protest to you, Gentlemen, that if I had to choose between a so-called University, which dispensed with residence and tutorial superintendence, and gave its degrees to any person who passed an examination in a wide range of subjects, and a University which had no professors or examinations at all, but merely brought a number of young men together for three or four years, and then sent them away as the University of Oxford is said to have done some sixty years since … I have no hesitation in giving the preference to that University which did nothing, over that which exacted of its members an acquaintance with every science under the sun.[15]

Better the university that brought young men of a certain class together under the right circumstances and in the right social and intellectual climate *and did nothing else* than the university that profligately 'gave its degrees to any person who passed an examination'.

As the idea of national culture lost its significance in public life, the university gradually shifted its emphasis to teaching and then to research, so that the purpose for which the Enlightenment university was originally established had, by the 1960s, been relegated to its 'third mission'. So, for example, the Robbins Report into higher education in the UK, published in 1963, outlined 'at least four objectives essential to any properly balanced system'.[16] The first two objectives related to training and education; the next, echoing Bacon, to 'the advancement of learning', that is, research; and the final one to 'the transmission of a common culture and common standards of citizenship', such that 'Universities and colleges have an important role to play in the general cultural life of the communities in which they are situated.'[15]

However, as the corporate ethos began to take hold in the university, the mission of public service was reconfigured accordingly. The Dearing Report,[18] from 1997, defined the concept of service almost entirely in economic terms, and by 2003 the UK government White Paper, *The Future of Higher Education*, shifted the rhetoric even further towards forging partnerships with local business. Thus, 'The best arrangements for working with business ... build a two-way process of higher education institutions and business learning about one another's needs and capabilities.'[19] As Carolyn Roper observed, 'the third mission has evolved from serving the community, to extending and reaching out to it, to engaging it in bi-directional relationships and interactions'.[20] This shift from public service to mutual gain through business partnerships was kick-started in the UK by a number of government initiatives in the late 1990s that reconfigured British universities as 'dynamos of growth' and 'major agents of economic growth'[21] and offered funding to support third-mission collaborations with business and industry. These financial incentives not only shifted the nature of the relationship between universities and the outside world onto a business footing, they also served to realign the disciplinary focus of the third mission from the arts and humanities to science and technology.

It could perhaps be argued that the newly revitalized third mission is nothing more than a pretext for justifying the wider corporate aim of income generation, and the increasing use by universities of phrases such as 'knowledge exploitation' and 'entrepreneurship' does little to allay such fears. In the case of my university, any potential business partnership must be 'sufficiently large in scale and scope', with an annual research turnover of at least £50 million being 'necessary to attract and retain companies to work alongside a university'. In addition, however, the focus and resources for developing these partnerships is channelled almost exclusively into the so-called STEM subjects of science, technology, engineering, mathematics and (sometimes) medicine. For my university, these subjects 'critically form the basis of the drive to expand the University's contribution to the knowledge economy and are the foundation for the development of the new Science and Innovation Campus'.[20]

We can see, then, that the original mission of the Enlightenment university has all but disappeared. The priorities of service, education and research have been reversed and corporatized and are driven by the goals of customer satisfaction, knowledge exploitation and financial reward. However, there are signs that the 'third mission', in its current guise of becoming 'a powerhouse for growth in the regional economy' by forming business partnerships with local industry, is growing in importance to the corporate university and has already overtaken the second mission of 'delivering an outstanding student experience'. This realignment of priorities can perhaps be discerned from my university's vision statement, cited earlier, which talks of research and wealth-creation but not of teaching and education.

The end of the university

Whilst there is no escaping the need for universities to become financially self-sufficient and even entrepreneurial, we should be aware of where these new priorities might lead us. The political philosopher Michael Oakeshott recognized the growing corporatization of the university more than 60 years ago, warning that:

> These ideas belong to a world of power and utility, of exploitation, of social and individual egoism, and of activity, whose meaning lies outside of itself in some trivial result or achievement... It is a very powerful world; it is wealthy, interfering and well-meaning. But it is not remarkably self-critical; it is apt to mistake itself for the whole world, and *with amiable carelessness it assumes that whatever does not contribute to its own purposes is somewhat errant.* A university needs to beware of the patronage of this world, or it will find that it has sold its birthright for a mess of pottage.[23]

Whilst this dangerous and perhaps unhealthy flirtation with the world of business is problematic, of far greater concern for the paraversity should be the 'amiable carelessness' that has resulted in the widespread rejection of the values of education and scholarship as 'somewhat errant', and which is currently leading to the systematic dismantling of the arts and humanities faculties in many universities.

The pressing need to subvert the mission of the corporate university therefore lies not so much in what the university has become as in what it has voluntarily given up in order to achieve the 'mess of pottage' that is corporate status. Oakeshott concluded his dystopic vision for the future of the university with the observation that:

> A university will have ceased to exist when its learning has degenerated into what is now called research, when its teaching has become mere instruction and occupies the whole of an undergraduate's time, and when those who came to be taught come, not in search of their intellectual fortune but with a vitality so unroused or so exhausted that they wish only to be provided with a serviceable moral and intellectual outfit; when they come with no understanding of the manners of conversation but desire only a qualification for earning a living or a certificate to let them in on the exploitation of the world.[24]

Based on these criteria, at least some universities in the UK (and I suspect elsewhere) no longer exist *as universities*, and the need to rethink the vision and the mission is urgent. I feel it necessary to emphasize once again, however, that I am not advocating a nostalgic return to some golden

Enlightenment age that had already all but passed when Oakeshott was writing in 1950. The corporate university is not going away anytime soon, and the only way forward is to adopt what Readings referred to as an 'institutional pragmatism' and a strategy of covert subversion from within by imposing a parallel vision for the university that focuses on quality and values.

Chapter 5

The fourth mission

'A man may think he has a "mission" in life, and he may think that his activity is governed by this "mission". But, in fact, it is the other way about; his missionary activity consists in knowing how to behave in a certain way and in trying to behave in that way; and what he calls his "mission" is only a shorthand expression of this knowledge and endeavor.'

Michael Oakeshott, *The Idea of a University*, 1950

The mission of subversion

The first step towards a new vision for the university is to subvert the very idea of a mission. Oakeshott expresses concern about the use of the terms 'mission' and 'function' in talking about what the university is for, because in his opinion universities are not *for* anything. Thus, 'A university is not a machine for achieving a particular purpose or producing a particular result; it is a manner of human activity.'[1] For Oakeshott, then, the 'mission' of the university has nothing to do with its function or with goals, but is simply the knowledge of 'how to go about the business of being a university', which involves 'knowledge of a tradition',[2] and which, even in 1950, he feared might already have been lost.

Whilst it is clearly not possible to reject completely the goals of the corporate university machine, we can at least undermine their intent and temper their worst excesses with the introduction of a 'fourth mission', the mission of the paraversity, based on Oakeshott's ideal of 'knowing how to behave in a certain way and in trying to behave in that way'. This fourth mission is therefore not concerned with outcomes, with targets or with scores. It does not set out principles for how best to conduct our research or educate our students and it does not propose a common end or particular methods and methodologies for achieving that end. In any case, the defining feature of the paraversity is that it is an organic, fluid, rhizomatic, evolving community of Thought that defies consensus and resists a single, simple solution to the question of how to open up a space for thinking, teaching and researching in the corporate University of Excellence. The fourth mission is concerned less with outcomes than, to borrow Oakeshott's somewhat quaint and archaic term, with the manners of conversation. That is to say, the mission of the paraversity is to establish a foundation of values and relationships necessary to build and sustain a rhizomatic community of Thought that encourages and enables us, as Deleuze and Guattari suggest, 'to move between things, establish a logic of the AND, overthrow ontology, do away with foundations, nullify endings and beginnings'.[3] This, of course, is the very antithesis of the stated mission of the corporate University of Excellence, and we might there-fore claim that the purpose of the fourth mission is to subvert the other three; that is, to influence them from below and to undermine them.

My proposal for a fourth mission is therefore the outline of a code of behaviour and a guide to manners for the paraversity, and as such it is open to interpretation by each individual member of the community of Thought. It is neither exhaustive nor definitive, and is offered merely as a suggestion and a starting point for thinking about how we might organize and conduct ourselves in a rhizomatic organization with no formally recognized leader-ship or management structure and no consensually agreed common goals. It is based on nothing more scientific and systematic than my own experiences in negotiating my way through the confines and strictures of the corporate University of Excellence and my observations of colleagues who have done, and are continuing to do, the same. Readings hoped that, 'after excellence', the university might become a site 'where the question of being together is raised'.[4] I have therefore divided the fourth mission, the subversive mission of the paraversity, into three exhortations, three responses to the question of being together. Clearly, I do not wish to imply a reductionist division or separation of any kind; the three elements of the mission of subversion do not relate to different aspects of my role, but suggest how I might conduct myself in relation to the university, to my colleagues, and to the discipline and practice of scholarship respectively. The fourth mission is therefore a personal, subjective and subversive response to the overt and collective corporate mission of the University of Excellence. For this reason, I will pres-ent it as a first-person-singular account from my own perspective and experience and invite the reader to take it or leave it as they see fit.

Be good

The first and perhaps the most subversive incitement of the mission of the paraversity is quite simply to *be good* in every sense of the word. It should, perhaps, go without saying that I should strive to be good in the moral and/or ethical sense, and the very fact that it needs to be said at all is a somewhat sad and sorry comment on the current state of the corporate university. Being good is concerned with knowing how to behave and with 'being together' at the institutional level; with my relationships, obligations and manners in regard to the structures and strictures of the corporate university. To be good in this context is to do the right thing, or perhaps to do the things that I consider to be right, or at the very least to do the things required of me by my university for the right reasons.

We can see immediately that being good is likely to come into conflict with being corporate. The injunction to be good is, first and foremost, an invitation to practise a values-based scholarship; that is, a scholarship based on a belief in the intrinsic value of the means and ends of teaching, research and service rather than on the extrinsic market value(s) of efficiency, the 'knowledge economy' and administration. Clearly, the corporate, outcome-driven agenda of the University of Excellence cannot be completely ignored: I must continue to contribute to the economic well-being of my university; I must work within the constraints of my contractual requirements, even if those requirements do not feature in the contract I originally signed up to when I took up employment with the institution; and I must also meet the largely quantitative and financially oriented Key Performance Indicators (KPIs) that have recently been imposed on me, largely without consultation or consent. The challenge, then, is to acknowledge and reconcile these conflicting corporate and scholarly agendas; if not to do the right thing, then at least to do the things required of me by the corporate university in the right ways and for the right reasons.

The values-based researcher

There are a number of ways in which I might respond to this challenge. If taken to its logical conclusion, the injunction to be good calls into question the very foundations on which my contractual and moral relationship with my university is constructed. However, a less contentious and disruptive approach to the challenge of being good would be to separate out the ends from the means, and to attempt to meet the outcomes of the corporate University of Excellence whilst remaining true to the values and methods of the paraversity. As a researcher, this might entail basing my decisions about which projects to engage with on considerations other than the size and source of available research grants or the journals in which the findings are likely to be published. For colleagues who, like me, work in applied or prac-tice-based disciplines, being a good researcher might mean placing the requirement to make a practical and substantive difference to the 'real' world beyond the confines of the academy above the requirement to satisfy the finance-driven metrics of research grants and publication impact factors. I might, for example, decide to apply for a small grant from a charitable organ-ization in order to conduct a research study with clearly defined local and practical outcomes rather than a larger and better-funded study designed to make a more general theoretical contribution to my discipline. I might employ 'soft' methodologies lacking in scientific rigour, such as participative action research or co-operative inquiry, which engage the eventual users of the research findings in a practical and productive reflexive partnership. And I might publish my research findings in journals that are read by members of a particular community of practice rather than in journals with high 'impact factors' that are read only by other academics and researchers and which are therefore less likely to have a direct impact on the outside world.

For academics who work in less-applied disciplines, the injunction to be good might be interpreted as the development of a programme of research that has personal value and meaning, which coincides with personal beliefs about how and to what end research should be conducted, or which promises to deliver outcomes and findings that are considered by the individual to have intrinsic or extrinsic value beyond the purely instrumental financial worth placed on research by the corporate university. It might also mean restricting the size and scope of research studies to a more human and humane level so that they are manageable by a single researcher or a small team rather than engaging in industrial-scale assembly-line projects that require a task-oriented division of labour and which depersonalize the process of doing research.

Clearly, it is far more difficult to meet the corporate research objectives that my university has set for me if my means and methods are determined by scholarly values rather than by directly addressing the quantitative measures of those objectives. For example, it is much easier for me to meet the corporate objective of scoring highly in the Research Excellence Framework (REF) if I only apply for large grants from prestigious funding organizations and if I only publish my papers in academic journals with high impact factors. That is not to say that it is impossible to meet the objectives of the corporate university in other ways, only that it is more difficult if I do not adopt an explicitly assessment-driven approach.

The values-based lecturer

The incitement to be good also applies to my role and activities as a lecturer, where taking a values-based approach might mean resisting the students' expectations that I will focus my teaching predominantly on helping them to pass their assignments. As with my research role, it might also mean resisting the expectations of my university that my primary concern will be to score highly on the various metrics by which 'excellent' teaching is measured, such as the UK National Student Survey, student attrition rates and the classification of degrees awarded. Rather than focus on the student experience, I might decide that my primary and fundamental role as a lecturer is to educate, and that education is not concerned with satisfying my students but with challenging them and perhaps even making them feel uncomfortable. I might decide that the purpose of teaching is not simply to impart information and facts in order to ensure that everyone passes their examinations. I might even work on the assumption that students do not come to university merely in order to learn (which requires neither a university nor a teacher) but to think, talk, argue, discover and create.

We have seen that, for Bill Readings, the purpose of what I refer to as the paraversity is to open up a space where staff and students might 'think together' without pressure to conform to any particular expectations or conclusions, where the didactic and/or dialectic one-way communication of information for the purpose of passing examinations is rejected in favour of a dialogic, communal construction of knowledge and understanding as part of the educational process itself. Whilst this approach to thinking and learning together as a community of dissensus might well provide a superior educational experience to the traditional lecture or, increasingly, the PowerPoint presentation, its superiority will not necessarily be translated into better examination results and lower attrition rates, or even, at least initially, into higher student-satisfaction scores.

The freedom to be good

Clearly, then, being good in the way that I have described it is not without risk. With job security in UK universities increasingly linked to performing well in metrics-based assessments such as the Research Excellence Framework, there is a potential conflict between bringing in research grants on the one hand and freely pursuing my own research programmes on the other; and between publishing in a limited number of high-impact-factor journals on the one hand and disseminating my findings widely and to my own chosen readership on the other. As the University and College Union (UCU) in the UK has warned, we are all under increasing pressure due to:

> the dominance of the Research Assessment Exercise [now the REF], the economistic (sic) approach of the Research Councils and growing pressures on academics to seek commercial sponsorship. Increasingly selective research funding puts pressure on academics to research in particular national priority areas, while commercialisation of research can restrict the timely dissemination of research findings into the public domain.[5]

There are similar risks involved in choosing to adopt an educational approach that does not set out explicitly to meet the metric targets imposed on me by the corporate university or to conform to a definition of 'excellence' that consists in little more than producing satisfied graduates with maximum efficiency and minimum wastage. Whilst my right to academic freedom[6] was enshrined in UK law by the Education Reform Act of 1988, this does not in itself offer cast-iron protection should I choose to be good rather than corporate. Thus, despite the fact that 'academic staff have freedom within the law to question and test received wisdom and put forward new ideas and controversial or unpopular opinions without placing themselves in jeopardy of losing their jobs or the privileges they may have',[7] the University and College Union is concerned that 'the freedoms to conduct research, teach, speak, and publish without interference or penalty, are increasingly under threat in UK universities and colleges',[8] to the extent that job security within the University of Excellence depends to some extent on conforming to the corporate agenda.

If I am to be good in the moral sense by subverting or refusing the demands of the corporate mission, it is therefore vitally important that I am also very good in the performative sense at what I chose to do in its place. The financially driven goals of my university still have to be met, and so I cannot base my relationship with the university on *moral values* without also addressing the question of *financial value*; or, as Readings puts it, I cannot raise questions of *academic accountability* without, to some extent, acknowledging the demand for *accountancy*. For Readings, then, the issue is 'how we can raise the question of accountability as something that exceeds the logic of accounting'.[9] Of course, I will almost certainly find it more difficult to achieve my key performance indicators if I choose to work outside the 'logic of accounting', and the injunction to be good must therefore be understood in its fullest sense of doing the right thing and doing it extremely well.

I might, however, take heart from the work of Richard Sennett, who invokes the somewhat neglected notion of craftsmanship and argues that quality arises from doing what we care about and what has meaning for us, without too much thought for the material gain that might or might not arise from it.[10] As we have seen, this is diametrically opposed to the corporate notion of quality, which equates it explicitly with quantifiable profit and gain. We need to have faith that those colleagues (for example, members of REF panels) who are making judgements about our teaching and research in relation to the financial rewards and academic kudos that it will bring to our universities will look beyond the metrics, and that good, high-quality work based on sound values will be recognized, valued and rewarded on its own merits.

Be collegiate

The second exhortation of the mission of the paraversity addresses my relationships with my colleagues and urges me simply to *be collegiate*. I have taken the term 'colleagues' in its wider sense to mean everyone with whom I interact on a day-to-day basis in the university, including administrators, students and other academics. I have excluded senior managers from this list since they have largely removed themselves from the day-to-day business and function of the organization and from the people who carry out that business, to the extent that they can no longer accurately be described as colleagues. Their place has been filled by a loose grouping of administrators, comprised of clerical, technical and (increasingly) former members of academic staff who were appointed to manage and facilitate the physical and human infrastructure of my school and the wider university.[11]

Administrators, academics and students

Whilst an ever-expanding administrative class is common to most bureaucratic organizations, it raises a number of issues for the paraversity. Of particular concern is the fact that these administrators are no longer simply organizing, but are increasingly making judgements and decisions that were previously made by academics about a variety of issues such as timetabling, room allocation and student assignments. Whilst these might, on the face of it, appear to be purely administrative matters, they have a profound impact on the provision and practice of education, and require at least a rudimentary understanding of educational and learning theories and an ongoing, day-to-day familiarity with the practicalities of teaching that many of these administrators do not possess. As Readings observes, 'the University of Excellence is one in which a general principle of administration replaces the dialectic of teaching and research, so that teaching and research, as aspects of professional life, are subsumed under administration'.[12] One important and far-reaching consequence of this shift in organizational power and responsibility for educational matters is that many of the metrics against which my teaching is assessed are now more or less completely beyond my influence. For example, the National Student Survey invites students to rate the courses on which I teach according to the effectiveness of the timetable, course organization, the communication of course and teaching changes, and access to library, IT and other resources. The assessment of my level of 'excellence' as a teacher is therefore, to some extent, based on the performance of administrators and managers.

At best, the relationship between academics and administrators has become confused and uncertain, and at worst it has fundamentally altered and perhaps reversed. Whereas in the Enlightenment university, the role of administrators was to support academics in the practice of education and research, the University of Excellence calls upon academics to support administrators in the smooth facilitation of students and research projects through the corporate machinery. Thus, academics are being judged and appraised more and more on their administrative skills and the extent to which they are prepared to place the business goals of the organization above the scholarly values of the academy.

The goals and pressures imposed by the University of Excellence have also fundamentally altered my relationships with fellow academics. Whilst the call for colleagues to be collegiate might once have been considered tautologous, I now regularly witness disputes between academic colleagues about whose names should be included on research papers, about the order in which those names should appear, about who 'owns' the publication for REF purposes and about who should be principal investigator on research grant bids. As Readings points out: 'Anyone who has spent any time at all in a University knows that it is not a model community, that few communities are more petty or vicious than University faculties.'[13] The sad fact is that our academic colleagues are now fierce competitors for increasingly scarce resources such as research grants, and first authorship of publications in the 'top' journals, as well as for the time needed to achieve these corporate outcomes. Thus, whilst the fashion for ever larger and more multidisciplinary research projects demands closer working relationships with a broad spectrum of academic colleagues, the growing culture of 'publish or perish' ensures that those relationships often have a ruthlessly competitive edge.

However, perhaps the greatest challenge to being collegiate lies in my relationships with my students. The traditional role of professors in relation to their students in the Enlightenment university has been that of *doctores* or *magisters* (masters) and *discipuli* (apprentices). Whilst not making any claims for academic or structural equity, the master–apprenticeship relationship was nevertheless collegiate and assumed obligations and responsibilities on both sides. In the corporate University of Excellence, this relationship has been recast as one of providers and purchasers of information and educational qualifications, placing students at the bottom of both the hierarchical organizational structure and the knowledge supply chain, and whose only obligation to the academic relationship is to pay their fees. In addition, the lowly role afforded to students as consumers rather than producers of knowledge and information has resulted in teaching being perceived by many academics as a second-rate activity that does not contribute directly to the knowledge economy and which often carries little or no weight when applying for promotion. This view has led growing numbers of academics to regard students as *personae non gratae* and their relationship with them as a distraction from the productive work of grant acquisition and research publication. At the same time, however, it is also recognized that, as customers, students wield a great deal of financial power and influence, and must therefore be kept 'satisfied'. The concept of a collegiate relationship between students and academics is therefore complex, problematic and, from a corporate perspective, not altogether desirable.

Rhizomes, machines and assemblages

The arborescent administrative structure of the University of Excellence not only controls and directs the flow of information but also the manner (and manners) of interactions between various groups and individuals. The apparently straightforward, linear, unidirectional, hierarchical administrative structure of the corporate university conceals a growing level of ambiguity and confusion in relation to power and status at all levels and between all groups. In particular, we have seen that administrators have assumed many of the functions previously carried out by senior managers and some aspects of the role of academics; students are finding themselves with an increasingly ambiguous status as, at the same time, customers, consumers and products of the higher education system; and the role of academics is more and more driven by competition to score highly on a series of banal, irrelevant and largely meaningless metrics. Taken together, these shifts in roles, responsibilities and expectations have corrupted and distorted the long-established networks and patterns of relationships of the traditional Enlightenment university and have resulted in disruptions and disjunctions to the very idea of collegiality.

Whilst there can be no return to the manners and relationships of the Enlightenment university, I have suggested that we must challenge and subvert the organizational and administrative structures that are exerting such a malign influence on how we relate to one another. In rethinking our collegiate relationships, we must therefore pay particular attention to the organizational and communication structures and networks at play in the paraversity. We have seen already that the arborescent organizational structure of the University of Excellence is rejected in the paraversity in favour of rhizomatic networks in which each individual constitutes a node that can, potentially, connect with any and all others. Rhizomatic networks blur and undermine the corporate distinctions in our roles and status and play down structural differences between academics, administrators and students. Communication across the paraversity is therefore (at least in principle) open, reciprocal and immediate, regardless of job title or position in the corporate hierarchy.

Deleuze and Guattari refer to the individual nodes of a rhizome as 'machines',[14] and point out that anything can constitute a machine: a person, a bicycle, a book, a camera or an art gallery. However, a machine has no closed identity in and of itself: 'it *is* nothing more than the connections and productions it makes; it is what it does'.[15] An art gallery is only a building until it is connected to one or more works of art. A bicycle has no 'meaning' until it forms a connection with a person; it then becomes a transportation machine (a vehicle) and the person becomes a cycling machine (a cyclist). If the bicycle had been connected to an art gallery rather than to a person, it would have become an artwork; if the person had been connected to a camera rather than to a bicycle, s/he would have become a photographer. Seen in this way, people only become academics when they are connected to books, to computers, to students, to administrators and to other academics to form temporary or semi-permanent networks and assemblages for specific purposes such as education, research, administration, project planning, curriculum writing or third-mission activities. At this point they become teaching machines, research machines, administrating machines or, more generally, thinking machines.[16]

Whilst these rhizomatic assemblages are, on the face of it, structurally and organizationally flat, it would be naive to imagine that issues of power simply disappear, particularly in the relationships between students and teachers. Indeed, Readings recognizes multiple sites of tension in these relationships and suggests that a seismic shift in the centre of power is required. Thus, 'in order to open up the question of pedagogy we do not need, therefore, to *recenter* teaching but to *decenter* it'.[17] That is to say, the educational rhizome does not shift the balance of power from (say) the professor to the student (a move which Readings refers to simply as *1968* in recognition of the student revolts in France of that year). Rather, to 'decenter' teaching is 'to refuse the possibility of *any* privileged point of view'[18] in favour of a dialogical relationship where students and academics 'think together' without any pressure or compulsion to arrive at consensus or for the student to satisfy specific predetermined knowledge outcomes. This move to 'decenter' teaching recognizes, with Foucault, that power resides not in individuals nor in appointed roles and positions, but in relationships, and that it ebbs and flows in all directions. We can therefore apply Readings' injunction to 'decenter' teaching to other assemblages and relationships, including research and administration.

From the perspective of the paraversity, the incitement to be collegiate can therefore be read as an invitation to connect, to 'plug in' and to form rhizomatic assemblages with colleagues and other machines in the lecture theatre, the research laboratory and the committee room. Being collegiate also carries certain responsibilities such as making ourselves available to a wide range of assemblages, paying attention to the connections between machines so as to keep them open and productive, encouraging the ebb and flow of power in all directions and ensuring that each machine in the assemblage is functioning as it should. In plain English, the injunction to be collegiate involves productive and effective networking with a wide range of colleagues (including administrators and students) on a variety of projects in a spirit of co-operation, generosity and openness. It means respecting the different experiences, views and perspectives that each member of the network (again including administrators and students) brings to the discussion and attempting to keep debates open and productive rather than imposing personal agendas or forcing a consensus.

Be radical

The third and final element of the mission of the paraversity addresses my relationship to the practice of scholarship and to my role as an academic, and urges me to *be radical*. In the face of the systematic dismantling of the Enlightenment university, and with it the traditional academic role, my relationship to scholarly practice entails, first and foremost, the duty and responsibility to prevent it from disintegrating and eventually disappearing.

The dis-integration of academic practice

At the heart of the problem is the unravelling (quite literally the dis-integration) of the university mission into its component strands in order to facilitate the smooth administration of research grants, students and entrepreneurial or business activity. As each aspect of the corporate mission has been operationalized and incentivized, academics have found it increasingly necessary to 'unbundle'[19] their work into its constituent parts of research, teaching, entrepreneurship and administration. This, in turn, has resulted in the creation within many university departments of discrete academic career streams intended to produce specialist researchers, teachers and entrepreneurs,[20] all overseen and organized by an administrative class of 'managers' (of people and departments) and 'directors' (of courses and programmes).[21] With financial issues taking on a growing significance and with government funding becoming more precisely targeted at 'centres of excellence', this segregation of missions and roles is being extended in the UK to a separation at the institutional level into teaching-only and research-only universities,[22] and even private 'business-only' universities.[23] On the one hand, the disintegration of the role and practice of the academic is a direct consequence of this separation of the mission and business of the university, but on the other hand, the passive acceptance of this academic apartheid is also facilitating and accelerating the demise of scholarship and the fully rounded academic.

The role, scope and job description of the academic has, of course, always been in flux in response to a variety of internal and external forces. For example, concerns during the 1980s centred on an increasing degree of subject specialism and a narrowing of disciplinary focus. As one commentator noted at the time, 'disciplines divided into sub-disciplines which were divided into specialities which were divided into "schools"'.[24] However, more recent developments have resulted in deep structural changes that have moved the debate beyond territorial disputes to threaten the integrity and perhaps the very existence of scholarship itself. Academics are, increasingly, being pressed to choose not only an ever narrower *subject area* but also a far more specific *mode of practice* in relationship to that subject, for example as a researcher, a teacher or an administrator. As Bruce Macfarlane recently observed, 'the traditional all-rounder who performs a combined teaching, research and service role is replaced by a series of specialists such as teaching or research-only appointees, instructional designers and assessors'.[25]

The incitement to *be radical* is therefore invoked in the face of a separation and segregation of the traditionally integrated and mutually supportive roles and components of academic practice, and should be understood in the fullest and most literal sense of the word. On the one hand, my dictionary informs me that to be radical is to take a bold and innovative approach marked by a considerable departure from the usual or traditional. On the other hand, being radical entails a consideration of the basic nature or composition of something and an examination of its roots or foundations (from the Latin *radix*). To take a radical approach to my practice therefore invites me to look again at the origin (perhaps even the essence) of what it means to be an academic and to find new and innovative ways of working in the face of a narrowing and disintegrating role.

Scholarship and the research–teaching nexus

The Janus-like challenge of how I might simultaneously look forward and backwards at my practice has been addressed, in part, in the work of the educationalist Lewis Elton. A recurring theme in Elton's writing has been a radical exploration of academic scholarship based on the principles outlined by Wilhelm von Humboldt, which led to the founding of the first 'modern' university in Berlin.[26] For Elton, Humboldt's 200-year-old blueprint for the modern university offers a way to reconcile the diverging roles of the academic through *Wissenschaft*, which Elton translates as 'scholarship', and which he suggests can 'build a bridge ("nexus") between research and teaching'.[27] The key to Elton's argument is what he refers to as Humboldt's 'central idea' that 'universities should treat learning always as consisting of not yet wholly solved problems and hence always in a research mode'.[28] Elton interprets 'learning in a research mode' (*forschendes Lernen*) as 'active and questioning in a way that traditional learning ... rarely is', and which demands from the teacher 'a deep and research-influenced understanding' of the learning process that he refers to as 'the scholarship of teaching and learning'.[29] Learning in a research mode therefore requires that I also *teach* in a research mode, and Elton claims that when applied in parallel, these radical approaches 'constitute the essence of the teaching–research nexus'[30] that 'helps to heighten the potential links between research and teaching'.[31]

The desire to forge links between teaching and research has been expressed at all levels and by all parties in the corporate University of Excellence as well as by those who are seeking alternatives to it. These attempts to create a nexus usually centre on a claim that doing research somehow informs and improves the practice of teaching (rarely the converse), although as Mark Hughes points out, such claims are based on a number of 'myths' about the 'mutually beneficial relationship between research and teaching'[32] that do not bear close scrutiny. Indeed, the desire to build a bridge between teaching and research might be seen as a tacit acknowledgement that they have been prised apart and are now widely regarded as separate and independent activities. From this perspective, Elton's proposal for *forschendes Lernen* as a nexus between the academic roles of teaching and research can only ever be a temporary measure in rescuing the idea and the practice of scholarship. As the teacher and the researcher grow ever more distanced from one another, to the extent even of working in separate specialized institutions, such bridges are in danger of becoming so extended that they collapse in the middle. In any case, whereas Elton's proposed (re)introduction of novel technologies of 'teaching in a research mode', such as enquiry-based learning and other discovery methods of learning, might address his agenda of bringing teaching and research closer together (or perhaps of ensuring that they do not move further apart), the more radical mission of the paraversity is fully to reintegrate them. And whereas Elton's engagement with Humboldt appears, at least in part to be a pragmatic attempt to adapt the latter's proposals to the realities of the corporate university of the twenty-first century,[33] the mission of the paraversity is one of resistance and subversion.

My reading of Humboldt therefore begins from a slightly different place and takes a slightly different perspective on the problem of scholarship. Whereas Elton sought (and found) in Humboldt's work a *nexus* or bridge that connects teaching with research, my understanding of Humboldt's *Wissenschaft* is that it acts not merely as a *nexus* but as a *plexus* in which teaching and research interweave to form a braid or a rhizomatic network; or perhaps even as a *fluxus* in which teaching and research flow together as two inseparable parts of a single process. Rather than *bridging* the gap between teaching and research, *Wissenschaft* offers a mechanism for *replacing* pure teaching (that is, the simple and straightforward unidirectional transmission of knowledge) and pure research (research that is detached from teaching and scholarship) with a reintegrated scholarship that blurs the distinctions between them.

Humboldt and the research–teaching plexus

When Humboldt wrote his treatise on intellectual institutions (*wissenschaftliche Anstalten*) at the turn of the nineteenth century, teaching and research in Germany were two very separate activities conducted by two separate groups of people in separate institutions, *universities* and *academies* respectively. Humboldt recognized, however, that the distinction was neither natural nor even planned. Rather, he argued that the system had 'developed in a haphazard way', and that to continue to regard teaching and research as distinct, separate and exclusive activities was 'partly wrongheaded and partly useless'.[34] Humboldt's call for the reform of what we would now call higher education was therefore an attempt to rethink the relationship between teaching and research, teachers and researchers, and universities and academies in the face of a very similar separation of roles and functions as we are now once again experiencing two centuries later. In a warning that is as relevant today as it was in Humboldt's time, he cautioned that 'the state must not deal with its universities as *gymnasia* [roughly translated as grammar schools] or as specialized technical schools; it must not use its academy as if it were a technical or scientific commission'.[35] In other words, institutions of higher education should not be regarded merely as places where students come to be trained for work and where funded research is conducted for purely technical or instrumental ends.

Humboldt's proposed solution was not, however, to bring universities and academies together, nor to build a bridge (nexus) between them, but rather to demonstrate that academies, those institutions concerned only with conducting research, could be dispensed with. Thus:

> If one assigns to the university the tasks of teaching and dissemination of the results of science and scholarship and assigns to the academy the task of its extension and advancement, an injustice is obviously done to the university. Science and scholarship have been advanced as much – and in Germany, even more – by university teachers as by members of academies.[36]

Humboldt's point was that teaching and scholarship, when conducted in the spirit of what Elton referred to as *forschendes Lernen*, is a superior form of research, and 'it is inconceivable that discoveries should not be frequently made in such a situation'.[37] Furthermore, whereas researchers in the academies had no access to students and therefore no opportunities to practise *forschendes Lernen*, university lecturers encountered no such barriers to conducting academic research. Thus, 'University teaching is moreover not such a strenuous affair that it should be regarded as a distraction from the calm needed for research and study; it is, rather, a help to it.'[38] Humboldt concluded: 'It would be entirely safe to entrust the growth of scientific and scholarly knowledge to the universities as long as they are properly conducted; *this is why the academies can be dispensed with*.'[39]

Humboldt is making two observations here. First, he is claiming that teaching, if conducted in a scholarly and inquiring manner, not only *transmits* knowledge but also *produces* it, and is therefore a powerful form of research. This was, in essence, the point that Elton took from Humboldt's work. Second, and far more radical, he is suggesting that pure research and dedicated researchers are not a necessary component of a university; that 'university teachers, quite without the establishment of their own academy, can achieve all the purposes assigned to an academy; they can form their own learned society...which is different from a genuine academy'.[40] That is not to say that there is no place for 'pure' decontextualised research in the university, only that it should not be its defining feature. There is no reason why universities should not compete with one another and with privately funded research institutes for grants to carry out contracted work. However, to elevate grant-capture to such heights that it becomes the most important criterion for academic promotion and, in some cases, the defining feature of the role of professor, is to undermine the very foundations of the university as an institution dedicated to education and scholarship.

Similarly, not all university teaching can ever meet Humboldt's criteria for *forschendes Lernen*, which he describes as 'a significant number of intelligences thinking in unison with the lecturer', and where 'problems are discussed back and forth by a large number of forceful, vigorous, youthful intelligences'.[41] The pressures placed on lecturers by having to teach larger and larger intakes of students, compounded by an increasingly assessment-driven curriculum and a 'publish or perish' culture means that the PowerPoint presentation of pre-prepared (often several years ago) bullet points and 'key facts' is now the teaching method of choice, and leaves little scope for discussion or debate. There are, of course, ways and means of engaging students in thoughtful discussions and intelligent debates, even when numbers are large and learning outcomes are narrowly defined. Elton suggests the need 'not just to use existing methods better, but to use better methods',[42] and identifies problem-based learning and other student-centred approaches as particularly useful and appropriate.

Clearly, different approaches and methods will be suitable for different disciplines and subjects, and it is beyond the scope and spirit of this book to offer a menu of student-centred teaching and learning strategies. What is important, however, and what we must not lose sight of, is that the injunction to be radical redefines my relationships with my students as that of partners (although, as Elton insists, not as *equal* partners) in the pursuit, production and dissemination of knowledge. As Humboldt points out:

> The relation between teacher and pupil at the higher level is a different one from what it was at the lower levels. At the higher level, the teacher does not exist for the sake of the student; both teacher and student have their justification in the common pursuit of knowledge.[43]

In contrast to education in schools, where the teacher's task is to 'present closed and settled bodies of knowledge',[44] the role of the lecturer 'at the higher level' is not to teach what is already known, but to engage with the student in an active exploratory and creative process of thought. This, of course, is more or less the same sentiment expressed by Bill Readings two centuries later when he proposed that teaching be 'decentred' so that teachers and students might 'think together' in dissensus without the pressure either for agreement or synthesis.[45]

Re-integrating the university

When Bill Readings surveyed the state of the Anglo-American university in the mid-1990s, he concluded that it was in ruins. My own assessment, nearly two decades later, is even bleaker. It seems to me that the commercial enterprise that the university has become is quite literally disintegrating into its component parts due largely to the administrative demand for specialist workers to take on responsibility for the delivery of the different elements of the university mission, each of which targets separate funding streams. The fragmentation and dis-integration of the university can be seen wherever we look, from the role of the individual academic to the organization and structure of the whole institution. At one end of the spectrum, we find academic subject specialists whose areas of expertise are so narrow that they have nothing to say even to colleagues in their own departments; researchers who do not teach; teachers who do no research; and administrators who do neither. At the other end, as funding for research is channelled into fewer and fewer 'centres of excellence', entire institutions are beginning to position themselves as teaching-only and research-only universities.

Whilst it seems quite clear to me that the very idea of a university without undergraduate students hardly qualifies for the title, there is also a growing concern that, in order to balance the accounts, the teaching-only universities will mostly revert back to being polytechnics and vocational training schools. Oakeshott warned as long ago as 1950 that:

> Somehow or another the idea of a University in recent years has got mixed up with notions such as 'higher education', 'advanced training', 'refresher courses for adults' – things admirable in themselves, but really very little to do with a university.[46]

If the university is to survive on the one hand as anything more than an institution for advanced training and refresher courses for adults, and on the other hand as merely a commercial firm of private research contractors competing for an ever-dwindling number of research grants,[47] then an urgent and radical reappraisal is required of the idea of the university and of the academic. This was the task that Readings set for himself, and one that I have attempted to expand and develop here.

Readings' response to the demise of the Enlightenment university of Culture was to suggest that we should dwell in its ruins in the spirit of dissensus, which entails 'thinking together' without pressure to conform or reach consensus, where the mission of the university, insofar as it has one, is simply to think, and where the product is nothing other than Thought itself. Towards the end of his book, Readings begins to sketch out some broad principles for how this commitment to thinking and Thought might be realized in terms of the traditional university activities of teaching and research. He suggests that we must resist the idea of the university as a corporate business dedicated to the production and sale of research findings and vocational qualifications, where 'what gets taught or researched matters less than the fact that it be excellently taught or researched',[48] and where 'excellence' is defined by administrators in terms of income-generation targets. However, he was the first to acknowledge that 'thinking what to do instead is more of a problem'.[49]

I have responded to Readings' challenge to think about 'what to do instead' with an outline of the paraversity as an invisible, subversive, virtual institution that runs alongside and in parallel to the corporate University of Excellence. In this final chapter of Part 2, I have attempted to subvert (that is to undermine) the mission of a dis-integrated, task-centred university as a commercial enterprise and to propose in its place a parallel 'fourth mission', which aims to reunite and reintegrate the vision, structure, people, relationships and activities of the academy as a rhizomatic network dedicated to the practice of radical scholarship. In the spirit of dissensus, I have tried not to be too prescriptive in how the idea of radical scholarship might be translated into the everyday activities and practices of the paraversity, preferring instead to focus on scholarship as what Oakeshott called 'a manner of human activity'.[50] In Part 3 I will examine more closely and in greater detail some of the structures and frameworks through which the human activity of the paraversity might be expressed.

Part 3

Adventures in the paraversity

'Fourier never describes his books as anything but the heralds of the perfect Book, which he will publish later (perfectly clear, perfectly persuasive, perfectly complex). The Annunciation of the Book (the Prospectus) is one of those dilatory manoeuvres which control our internal utopia. I imagine, I fantasize, I embellish, and I polish the great book of which I am incapable: it is a book of learning and of writing, at once a perfect system and the mockery of all systems, a summa of intelligence and of pleasure, a vengeful and tender book, corrosive and pacific, etc. (here, a foam of adjectives, an explosion of the image-repertoire); in short, it has all the qualities of a hero in a novel: it is the one coming (the adventure), and I herald this book that makes me my own John the Baptist, I prophesy, I announce...'

Roland Barthes, *Roland Barthes by Roland Barthes*, 1977

I would like, just for a moment, to anticipate where Part 3 of this book is heading (after all, is that not the function of an introduction – to prepare the readers for what they are about to read? Or, as Derrida puts it, 'Here is what I wrote, then read, and what I am writing that you are going to read'[1]). In what you are now about to read, the paraversity will be compared to the book, to a certain kind of book, in terms of its structure, its authorship and the process of reading it. As with Fourier's 'perfect Book', the danger persists that this book will never be written, that the paraversity will never be built; that all I (we) am capable of is the 'Annunciation of the Book (the *Prospectus*)', merely another addition to the long line of 'heralds of the perfect Book' that we will publish later. The more that I (we) fantasize, embellish and polish 'the great book of which I am incapable', the more distant it seems, the more likely it is that it will forever be nothing more than (to once again anticipate what is to come in Part 3) an imaginary book, an unrealized project (although, as we shall see, even imaginary books can assert a certain amount of influence).

In the previous chapter, I concluded that the university is both literally and figuratively disintegrating before our eyes, and that we need urgently to think again about what we might wish to see in its place; that is to say, how we might regain the idea of scholarship in a corporate, commercial institution. I suggested that a realistic starting point might be with a new, subversive mission; a scholarly mission that subverts *the very idea* of a mission. In Part 3, I venture a few further thoughts on this adventure, this *adventus*, this coming into being. In places and at times these thoughts might be perceived as just a little too prescriptive, as *already written*. This is not my intention: the following three chapters are not offered as a prescription for how to behave in the paraversity; they are not instructions about what to do, or even what to think, but serve only as a reminder that we *must* think, and think differently, if we hope to work differently. With Richard Rorty, my aim throughout this book, but particularly in Part 3, has been 'to redescribe lots and lots of things in new ways'[2] in the hope and expectation that thought follows language, and that writing and speaking in new ways might lead eventually to acting in new ways. Part 3, then, takes Rorty's advice and

> says things like 'try thinking of it this way' – or more specifically, 'try to ignore the apparently futile traditional questions by substituting the following new and possibly interesting questions'.[3]

What, then, can we do in order to realize the paraversity? That, surely, is one of the futile traditional questions that Rorty encourages us to ignore. We can do as we please and what pleases us: something old, something new, something borrowed . . . The question is not *what* we do, but *how* we might do it, and my answer is that, whatever we do, we should try to be good, collegiate and radical in our intentions.

Part 3 outlines some thoughts on a new scholarship for the paraversity structured around the three activities of writing, teaching and reading, whilst acknowledging, of course, that they are all intimately connected. In Chapter 6, I raise some 'new and possibly interesting questions' concerning how and what we might write and publish in the name of scholarship, and suggest that 'writing an essay', which Readings took as a metaphor for thinking in the university, might be enacted in a more literal way (in fact, I attempt [*essayer*] to enact it myself in two essays on the essay). Chapter 7 raises questions about teaching, learning, education and knowledge, and speculates about what (if anything) teaching is *for*, and how it might best be conducted. I propose a return to the seminar, not as a specific practice but as a way of thinking again about knowledge and the kinds of learning and teaching appropriate to the pursuit of knowledge. In the final chapter I turn my attention to reading, and in particular to the practice of 'reading a book' as a metaphor not only for scholarly activity but also for the paraversity itself. This book ends, as it began, with the work of Bill Readings and a commitment to reading as a moral and practical act dedicated to the process of thinking together in a community of dissensus.

Chapter 6

On the essay

'In the emphatic essay, thought gets rid of the traditional idea of truth.'
Theodor Adorno, *The Essay as Form*, 1958

Writing and the production of knowledge

The 200-year history of the modern university is a catalogue of compacts and contracts with the state, initially to safeguard and propagate national culture, and latterly to contribute to the local and national economy and to train graduates for the job market. The idea of the university has therefore altered substantially from Humboldt's ivory tower of 'freedom and the absence of distraction'[1] to the recently stated mission of my own university to become 'a powerhouse for growth in the regional economy'.[2] Hence, one of the major claims made in this book is that the vision and the mission of the university has shifted from the production and dissemination of thought and ideas to the generation and sale of facts and data, largely in response to what Lyotard has referred to as the growing 'mercantilization of knowledge'.[3] As the production of raw, generalizable, 'useful'[4] information replaces the disinterested pursuit of nuanced and contextualized knowledge, the question for the corporate University of Excellence becomes one of how this new commodity might best be (re-)presented, packaged, communicated and (increasingly) sold in the marketplace of the so-called knowledge economy.

Lyotard first addressed this question in the late 1970s in a 'Report on Knowledge' commissioned by the University Council of the government of Quebec.[5] Lyotard claimed that, in the post-industrial age, technical knowledge and information has become increasingly important to the nation-state to the extent that 'Knowledge in the form of an informational commodity indispensable to productive power is already, and will continue to be, a major – perhaps the major – stake in the worldwide competition for power.'[6] Drawing on the work of Wittgenstein, he identifies the narrative or story as the medium through which knowledge and ideas are formulated and communicated, and points out that narrators engage with their audiences in a variety of 'language games' in order to explore complex ideas and propositions from a number of contrasting and conflicting perspectives. Depending on the language game or games being employed, narrative accounts of knowledge might include (among others) *denotative* statements that tell or inform, *deontic* statements that prescribe what should be done, *interrogative* statements that challenge and invite choices, and *evaluative* statements that offer judgment and critique.[7]

In a world where, increasingly, knowledge cannot be separated from power,[8] where commercial and political interests overlap, and where control over the production and dissemination of this 'informational commodity' is crucial, it is of vital importance to the nation-state and its institutions that the currency of the knowledge economy is stable and strong. Narrative forms and language games that weaken the currency by challenging, evaluating and calling into question the status or truth-value of knowledge and the accuracy of information are therefore played down and actively discouraged, and the language game of denotation, the straightforward authoritative *telling* of the facts through PowerPoint presentations and scientific reports is now widely regarded as the predominant mode of the representation and dissemination of knowledge.

The corporate University of Excellence has responded to this demand from industry, commerce and the state for stability and certainty in a number of ways. First, there has been a gradual shift in the role of the academic from raising questions to providing answers; from problematizing to problem-solving.[9] Second, there has been a move away from the spoken word as the preferred medium for the presentation of academic knowledge and information in favour of written text that has a tangible, physical presence and can be copyrighted, published, stored and sold.[10] Taken together, these external pressures and demands for solid facts and hard data have resulted in the elevation by the corporate university of the denotative written report as its most highly regarded output, and the subsequent devaluation of other more discursive or speculative narrative forms such as the conference presentation, the scholarly symposium, the discussion paper, the polemic and the essay. This shift in the values and priorities of the university from pursuing knowledge to conveying information and facts is enacted internally by the growing emphasis on performance indicators, such as well-cited scientific papers as the measure of the 'quality' of the work of the academic, and externally in the privileging by journal editors and book publishers of denotative writing such as the research report and the textbook.

Writing and method

Whereas the role of the academic in the Enlightenment university has traditionally included speculation, innovation and creative thinking, the primary purpose of the report and the textbook is to convey information as precisely, unambiguously, unequivocally and authoritatively as possible, and this presents the academic writer with two novel challenges. First, there is the problem of legitimation, of convincing the reader that the message is accurate and true. Lyotard suggests that the credibility of the narrative traditionally depends partly on a judgement by the audience about its content, and partly on the audience recognizing and accepting the narrator as competent, credible and (in some cases) qualified to convey the message. In other words, writers must not only be authorities in their academic fields, but they must also be recognized by colleagues as such. However, Lyotard points out that the scientific report is almost unique amongst the variety of narrative forms available to us in that it carries within itself its own legitimating story or *metanarrative*.[11] The academic report or write-up usually includes not only information about the subject at hand, but also a narrative addressing the question of why that information must be accepted as true. This will generally be in the form of an appeal to methodology, either the scientific method or, in the arts and humanities, the current dominant theoretical perspective. The academic report delivers a twin message: it says, in effect, 'X is true and these are the reasons why it must be accepted as true.' Its validity or truth-claim is therefore universal and depends neither on the perceived authority of the writer nor on the subjective judgement of the reader, but only on an objective demonstration of the correct application of method.[12]

The appeal to method brings with it a second challenge for the report writer. If the credibility of the information depends largely on the correct application of method, then the procedure must be described straightforwardly and transparently, and in a way that can be compared with and judged alongside other reports against an external gold standard of best practice. This is usually achieved by adopting a prescribed common format (headings and subheadings, which may vary from discipline to discipline), an impersonal 'objective' style (third-person or passive case) and a single denotative language game of telling. Academic reports or write-ups therefore tend towards simple statements of fact presented in a straightforward, authoritative, instructional form, structure and style. As Lyotard adds:

> Of course, we find other classes of statements, such as interrogatives ('How can we explain that...?') and prescriptives ('Take a finite series of elements...'). But they are only present as turning points in the dialectical argumentation, which must end with a denotative statement. In this context, then, one is 'learned' if one can produce a true statement about a referent...[13]

That is to say, being seen as 'learned' now depends far more on the ability to write in an *authoritarian* style rather than in an *authoritative* one. Furthermore, this association between being 'learned' and the production and dissemination of statements of empirical truth suggests that the rules and procedures of scientific report-writing have spilled over into the wider academy, where laboratory values such as rigour, control and detachment are increasingly being applied to academic writing in all disciplines, including the arts and humanities.

The application of these values outside of the laboratory is not a new phenomenon. We need look no further than the flirtation of the French literary critics with structuralism in the 1950s and 1960s to see how the methods and procedures of science can be applied to artistic judgement. For example, Roland Barthes proposed Saussure's semiology as 'a science of forms',[14] and proceeded to develop it during the 1950s into a complex method for the structural analysis of literary works (and later, other art forms such as photography, architecture, cinema, and so on), complete with technical terminology, diagrams and equations.[15] As late as 1967, Barthes was still making comparisons between science and literature:

> Like science, literature is methodical; it has its programs of research, which vary according to schools and periods (like those of science, moreover), its rules of investigation, sometimes even its experimental pretensions.[16]

However, by this time he was beginning to question the relevance of scientific values and method to the study of literature and urged 'for the structuralist to transform himself into a "writer"'.[17] Thus:

> objectivity and rigor, attributes of the scholar which we still hear so much about, are essentially preparatory virtues, necessary to the work's moment, and as such there is no reason to mistrust them or to abandon them; but these virtues cannot be transferred to discourse, except by a kind of hocus-pocus.[18]

By the early 1970s, Barthes had abandoned completely any scientific pretensions for literary writing and criticism, claiming that Method (his use of upper case) is sterile and objectivity is largely an illusion.[19]

Writing in the paraversity

It would appear, then, that the desire for method, rigour and objectivity ebbs and flows over time and throughout the academy. However, their coming in and falling out of favour has in the past been prompted by theory and ideology (hence the cyclical pattern), whereas their growing popularity in the corporate University of Excellence is underpinned and driven not by intellectual theory but by commerce, industry and the desire by universities to produce a saleable commodity. This is an altogether more worrying prospect from the point of view of the paraversity, and one that demands a response.

I have suggested in this book that the aim and mission of the paraversity is to subvert the corporate agenda of the University of Excellence and to replace it with a commitment to what Bill Readings calls dissensus and 'thinking together'. Readings proposes the *essay* as the mode of writing most suited to the needs, purposes and mission of the paraversity, and adds that '"writing an essay" is, of course, a metaphor here, a metaphor for producing a judgment of value that seeks to grapple with and take responsibility for itself as a discursive act',[20] and where 'Judgment is better understood in relation to a continuing discussion rather than as a finality'.[21] To write an essay is therefore to engage in an ongoing, open-ended discussion in, with and about the academy, and stands in stark contrast to the closed, authoritarian, unidirectional denotative style of the report in a number of ways.

First, the purpose of writing a report is to tell or impart information as straightforwardly and unambiguously as possible, whereas the purpose of writing an essay is to discover or create. Barthes (having completed the transition from structuralist to post-structuralist) claims that '"Research", then, is the name which prudently, under the constraint of certain social conditions, we give to the activity of writing',[22] to which Max van Manen adds that 'writing teaches us what we know, and in what way we know what we know', such that 'not until we had written this down did we quite know what we knew'.[23] We can therefore distinguish between two quite different forms of writing, which we might call *writing-up* research and *writing-as* research. Second, the mode of communication of the report is didactic, unidirectional and impersonal. As a meta-narrative, it does not depend on its readership for validation or legitimation, and is therefore simply a monologue transmitted into the ether.[24] In contrast, the essay is dialogical, discursive and speaks directly to the individual reader. It requests, cajoles and solicits support for its ideas and attempts to engage the reader in an ongoing debate. Whereas the report keeps the reader at a distance, the essay (re)instates the reader as an active participant in the process of writing. If writing an essay entails the active creation of knowledge, then it is an act of creation that involves both reader and writer, and we might therefore refer to these two modes of communication respectively as writing *at* the reader and writing *with* the reader. Finally, whereas the report is regarded as a transparent medium for the objective conveyance of external content and information, the essay is reflexive; it turns its attention back onto itself and its writer; it is (usually) a first-person account that often tells the reader as much about its author as about its subject matter. To write an essay is, unavoidably, to write oneself.

Essaying the essay

Adorno regards the essay form as closely related to rhetoric, 'which the scientific mentality, since Descartes and Bacon, has always wanted to do away with'.[25] Even in 1958, he recognized that 'the relevance of the essay is that of an anachronism' and that it is being crushed by an 'organized science . . . in which everyone presumes to control everyone and everything else'.[26] As Graham Good more recently added, 'The essay opposes doctrines and disciplines, the organizing structures of academic knowledge.'[27] The question and the challenge for the paraversity is thus how to argue for the essay in an institution and at a time where its virtues are no longer recognized or appreciated; how to present a convincing argument to the academy against everything that it has come to value.

I am therefore faced with a dilemma: do I present my case in the form, style and structure that I wish to argue against, or do I make the case for the essay *as an essay*? In the first instance, my work would have a far greater chance of being published and read by those to whom I wish to make my case. It might be argued that my best chance of persuading and convincing academics of the virtues of the essay form is to address them in the language, style and mode of debate with which they are most familiar and comfortable; that is, to tell or inform them about the essay through a rational, well-ordered, well-referenced, logical presentation of the facts. On the other hand, the pragmatist philosopher Richard Rorty suggests, with Wittgenstein, that most philosophical debates are not arguments of any substance but merely disputes over the meaning of words. The difficulty with attempting to argue for a particular language game (say evaluation or interrogation) using the structures and vocabulary of a different one (in this case denotation) is that words and phrases are taken out of context and ascribed unintended meanings by the reader. The problem, as Rorty sees it, is that 'The trouble with arguments against the use of familiar and time-honored vocabulary is that they are expected to be phrased in that very vocabulary.'[28] Any argument against the vocabulary or academic form that I am writing in, therefore, 'is bound to be inconclusive and question-begging',[29] since it will be phrased in the very language game that I am attempting to supplant.

According to Rorty, then, I cannot present a strong and convincing argument for the essay using the vocabulary and language game of the academic report; there are no logical or 'scientific' arguments to be made for a mode of writing that largely eschews logic and science. To paraphrase Harold Bloom, the meaning of an essay can only be another essay.[30] Rorty's method is therefore not to offer rational argument or logical reasoning, but 'to redescribe lots and lots of things in new ways, until you have created a pattern of linguistic behaviour which will tempt the rising generation to adopt it.' He continues:

> This sort of philosophy does not work piece by piece, analyzing concept after concept, or testing thesis after thesis. Rather, it works holistically and pragmatically. It says things like 'try thinking of it this way' – or more specifically, 'try to ignore the apparently futile traditional questions by substituting the following new and possibly interesting questions'.[31]

He concludes:

> Conforming to my own precepts, I am not going to offer arguments against the vocabulary I want to replace. Instead, I am going to try to make the vocabulary I favour look attractive by showing how it may be used to describe a variety of topics.[32]

Rorty is suggesting that a persuasive case for the essay can only be made by writing an essay. However, this approach carries the risk, particularly in the more scientific disciplines, that it will never be published where it will be read by its intended audience.

From the perspective of the corporate University of Excellence and the arborescent logic of 'either-or',[33] I am faced with the dilemma of choosing the best or most effective mode of presentation in which to convey knowledge and facts about the essay. However, I have suggested that the paraversity is structured around the rhizomatic logic of the AND, 'where thought takes place beside thought'[34] without the need or pressure to converge on a definitive conclusion. In the spirit of rhizomatic thought, I will therefore attempt (*essayer*) to present the case for the essay *both* in the form of the traditional academic paper *and* in the style of the essay. In my first attempt, I will employ references and citations from a range of published sources as voices of authority to argue that such citations are not always appropriate or relevant to the essay form. In the second, I restrict direct citations from other writers to a few memorable quotes 'only to make myself more explicit'.[35] The first attempt offers a semblance of balance and objectivity in its argument against balance and objectivity, whilst the second is blatantly and unashamedly partisan in its views and opinions. The first attempt is structured according to the usual academic conventions of subheadings, whereas the second is presented as a continuous flow of prose. The first is an appeal to rationality and to logic, the second to reason and rhetoric. However, the attentive reader will notice that each arrives, by a somewhat different route, at the same conclusion.

First attempt: an experiment in thinking[36]

> 'If my mind could gain a firm footing, I would not make essays, I would make decisions; but it is always in apprenticeship and on trial.'
>
> Michel de Montaigne, *Essais*, 1580

The essay form

It is generally agreed that the essay form was conceived by the French writer Michel de Montaigne, who coined the term *essais* in the mid-sixteenth century from the French *essayer*, meaning to try, attempt or test. For

Montaigne, to write an essay was to try out ideas or test thoughts in relation to a particular topic. In its classic form, the essay is typically written in the first-person singular and presents the opinions and subjective viewpoint of the writer.[37] It is often an experiment with new ideas and is therefore a formative rather than an instructive enterprise. As Montaigne observed, 'I speak as one who questions and does not know...I do not teach, I only relate.'[38] The essay is therefore not intended as a way of instructing others about what we already know, but rather as a *creative exercise* in order to discover for ourselves what we *think we might think* about a particular topic. Lukács,[39] writing in 1911, suggested that the essay is a literary form, midway between poetry and philosophy. The essayist deals with substantive issues in the manner of the philosopher but, like the poet, places great emphasis on the form and language in which those issues are addressed. Thus, for Lukács, the point in writing an essay lies 'not in the verdict...but the process of judging';[40] not in the conclusion but in the thinking and the writing that leads to the conclusion. Similarly, Barthes[41] considers the possibility that 'to write' can be employed as an intransitive verb, a verb with no object. It is less important what we write *about* than it is simply to write.

The essay as literary form has enjoyed a long and distinguished history, but partly due to a reduction in suitable publishing formats, it has fallen out of favour in recent years.[42] The term 'essay' is now used mostly in an academic context, and essays are written predominantly by students rather than professional academics. As Bakewell observes:

> Today, the word 'essay' falls with a dull thud. It reminds many people of the exercises imposed at school or college to test knowledge of the reading list: reworkings of other writers' arguments with a boring introduction and a facile conclusion stuck into each end like two forks into a corn-cob.[43]

In many disciplines, the essay has become a mechanical exercise in which the student is required to write in the third person or the passive case, to stick to the facts, to avoid personal opinion and to support all assertions with up-to-date references from the academic literature. In a similar vein, Good considers the student essay to be restricted by the personalized and limited cache of knowledge of the individual writer, and therefore regards it as a 'preliminary form...of use only until the student has acquired enough impersonal knowledge to write research papers and perhaps eventually scholarly articles, where the personal element is minimized'.[44] In either case there is general agreement that the essay form is suitable only for students and nascent academics and is of little consequence to the academy and those who work in it.

Clearly, the literary essay as conceived by Michel de Montaigne and the student essay as described by Good and Bakewell are two quite separate and distinct forms, and perhaps their only point of similarity is the term 'essay' itself. Whereas the student essay is a preliminary attempt or 'try' (*essayer*) at an academic piece of work, the literary essay is an experiment or 'trying out' of new ideas; whereas students typically write essays in order to demonstrate to the marker what they already know, the literary essay is an attempt to create new knowledge; and whereas the student presents the work of other writers, personal essayists are predominantly writing their own thoughts and ideas. Regardless of these differences, neither the student essay nor the literary essay are recognized and accepted academic forms, and neither typically meets the standards usually required for publication in an academic journal.

The academic essay

However, between the literary essay and the student essay lies the third way of the academic essay. The academic essay is closer to the former than the latter; it usually takes the form of a personal first-hand account, it is passionate and frequently adversarial, and it is unashamedly partisan and one-sided. However, in common with the student essay, it often draws on the wider academic literature, although not in any systematic way, and sometimes without explicitly citing its sources. Whereas most academic writing, including the student essay, employs 'an apparatus of citations and references which bind it into the "textuality" of its discipline',[45] academic essayists traditionally draw on their own reading experience, often quote from memory and expect their readers to be familiar with the citations. Thus, 'There are often quotations in the essay, but rarely footnotes.'[46]

However, in light of a number of recent high-profile accusations of plagiarism, such an expectation is no longer reasonable, and there is an increasing trend for citations in academic essays to be formally referenced.[47] Nevertheless, there is little attempt at a systematic review or a comprehensive account of the literature. The academic essay 'does not begin with Adam and Eve but with what it wants to discuss; it says what is at issue and stops where it feels itself complete – not where nothing is left to say'.[48] The purpose of citations and quotations is not to lend external authority to the essay: 'Thought acquires its depth from penetrating deeply into a matter, not from referring it back to something else',[49] and ultimately, 'an essay can become authoritative in academia partly because it does not cite authorities and speaks on its own authority'.[50] When the work of other writers *is* quoted, it is usually as 'a way of bringing a new voice into the conversation, rather than providing authoritative support'.[51] In Montaigne's words, 'I quote others only to make myself more explicit.'[52]

The essay as experiment

The essay performs a number of important functions in and for the academy. Firstly, the essay makes knowledge claims in the same vein as, but distinct from, the scientific research paper. The essay differs from the research paper in form, method and content. Its form is discursive, lop-sided and unstructured: 'In the essay, concepts do not build a continuum of operations, thought does not advance in a single direction, rather the aspects of the argument interweave as in a carpet.'[53] To a large extent, the form of the academic essay is determined by the method, or perhaps by the *lack* of method. In Adorno's words, the essay proceeds 'methodologically unmethodologically',[54] that is, its method is to follow the twists and turns of the train of thought that it is seeking to express. In fact, the form and method of the essay is best defined in terms of what it stands against, which is scientific empiricism and the quest for certainty. In its place, the essay offers rhetoric that has, since the time of Plato, been positioned in opposition to logic and rationality. The method of rhetoric relies on persuasive argument rather than statement of empirical facts; it says 'try thinking about it in this way' rather than 'this is the way it is'. Whereas the scientific paper *presents* its conclusions, the essay engages the reader in a *discussion* and invites a response; whereas the scientific paper *reports* its method and findings, the essay *is* the method and findings. It might therefore be argued that the essay fulfils the functions of both the research project *and* the research report. In this sense, the essay is no less experimental than the method of science; it is simply that the experimentation and the discovery occur in the act of writing itself. As Bense observes:

> Thus the essay distinguishes itself from a scientific treatise. He writes essayistically who writes while experimenting, who turns his object this way and that, who questions it, feels it, tests it, thoroughly reflects on it, attacks it from different angles, and in his mind's eye collects what he sees, and puts into words what the object allows to be seen under the conditions established in the course of writing.[55]

The essay form is therefore a method for the more or less spontaneous creation of knowledge, although it is knowledge of a different kind from that produced by empirical research. The knowledge produced by essayistic writing does not form part of an organized whole; it cultivates diversity rather than unity, and it is founded in the experience of the writer rather than in the scientific research project. Furthermore, it only *fully* becomes knowledge when the reader begins to interact with it. The essay is, in effect, one side of an open-ended discussion between writer and reader, and the scope and extent to which the essay generates knowledge is therefore largely dependent on the number and nature of its readers and their willingness to engage with and respond to the text. As Bakewell says of Montaigne's *Essays*, it 'is much more than a book. It is a centuries-long conversation between Montaigne and all those who have got to know him.'[56] As well as performing the dual function of simultaneously creating knowledge and reporting on it, the essay therefore also seeks to engage the reader as a literal or metaphorical co-writer.

The essay as critique

As well as a method for generating knowledge, the essay offers a vehicle for critique. Alter notes that the word 'essay' is also related to 'assay', to weigh up or analyse,[57] and Adorno adds that the essay is 'the critical form *par excellence*'.[58] However, its mode of critique is not the conservative 'university criticism' identified by Barthes,[59] which merely judges according to the agreed and accepted academic standards of the day. Rather, both the form and content of the essay implicitly undermine the unifying project of the academy by privileging the singular, the diverse and the personal. As Good points out, 'the essay opposes doctrines and disciplines, the organizing structures of academic knowledge – hence the essay's neglect in the higher levels of the academic literary system'.[60] The essay transgresses subject boundaries; it blurs form and content, subject and object, theory and praxis, in ways that contravene many of the traditional rules and practices of 'good' university scholarship. The essay challenges what Barthes refers to as the *doxa*, the body of accepted academic opinion that 'goes without saying',[61] both in what it says and in the form it adopts in order to say it. Essayistic critique might therefore be described as *radical* insofar as it attacks the very roots (*radix*) on which the academy is founded.

The essay as resistance

The essay offers a form (albeit a loose one) that encourages us not only to *write* differently, but to *think* differently; to think in an undisciplined way; that is, unfettered by the usual disciplinary constraints. Adorno emphasizes this important connection between thinking and writing in his claim that 'The essay is the form of the critical category of our mind'.[62] The essay is therefore a written expression, perhaps *the* written expression, of radical thought, and as such it provides a public forum for dissent that is not constrained by the forms and structures that it is arguing against. Adorno appears to be suggesting that all radical critique tends towards the essay form, and perhaps even that the essay form is essential to the formulation and expression of critique. If this is indeed the case, then any discipline that rejects the essay as unscholarly or even as anti-academic is also excluding the possibility of a fundamental radical critique of itself.

Barthes would no doubt have argued that this is precisely the point – that the rejection of the essay as an academic form is an attempt to restrict challenges to the *doxa*, to reinforce existing disciplinary structures and boundaries and thereby to maintain ownership and control over the generation and dissemination of disciplinary knowledge. It is perhaps worth remembering that the academic use of the terms 'doctrine' and 'discipline' originate in the Latin *doctor* (teacher) and *discipulus* (student or disciple). A challenge to the academic system of doctrines and disciplines is therefore a direct challenge to the ethos of leaders and disciples and hence to the hierarchical structure of the ownership and dissemination of knowledge. It could therefore be argued that there is far more at stake than merely the reinstatement of what might be seen by some as a somewhat archaic academic form. It is perhaps no coincidence that the demise (or perhaps the suppression) of the academic essay has been accompanied by a subsequent rise in the academy of corporatism, managerialism and performance indicators. The essay, then, is the subversive voice of the paraversity.

Second attempt: just writing

'The meaning of a poem can only be another poem.'
Harold Bloom, *The Anxiety of Influence*, 1973

If, as Readings suggests, 'writing an essay' is a metaphor for producing a judgement, then both 'writing' and 'essay' signify vast areas for study and thought whose surfaces have barely been scratched. We know from the dictionary that an essay is a short piece of prose writing on a specific topic, and that it is also an effort or an attempt, especially an initial or tentative one; and we know, in addition, that the word has its roots in the French *essayer* – to try – and perhaps in the Latin *exagium* – to weigh.

The essay as an attempt at weighing up or judging might once have been considered almost as a metaphor for the university itself, but speculative attempts and judgements are no longer regarded as suitable activities even for students, let alone for academics. Universities are no longer places where students come to be educated, reared (*educatus*) or cultivated (*cultus*), where they might develop their judgements and 'try out' their thoughts and ideas for life. The rise in popularity of the 'gap year' can perhaps be regarded as an acknowledgement that if young people wish to acquire an education in the classical sense of the word, then they should attend to it before coming to university. University is now associated with preparation for the world of work rather than as a place where students might study, to borrow Humboldt's expression, in 'freedom and seclusion [*Einsamkeit*]', insulated (if only for a while) from the distractions associated with earning a living. As such, its purpose is to provide students with the knowledge, skills and qualifications necessary for gainful employment rather than to cultivate them as individual minds and intellects.[63]

The success of the university in achieving these goals is measured by the ability of students to reproduce this vocational knowledge in a prescribed written format by following an established process or protocol. They are thus also taught the value of discipline and rigour; that if they rigorously and rigidly apply the appropriate (predetermined) method they will arrive at the correct conclusion. And, of course, they learn that whilst a number of possible conclusions might be drawn from any collection of facts or data, some are more correct than others. In other words, students are taught not only the knowledge and information that they will need to pursue their chosen profession, but also the 'transferable lifeskills' of rigorously following prescribed procedures in order to arrive at predetermined conclusions that are essential for junior employees starting out in almost *any* new job.

It will, of course, be pointed out that students continue to write essays in which they are required to weigh up the facts and arrive at judgements in the form of conclusions; and that academics, whilst rarely writing formal essays, also pass judgement in the name of commentary, critique and evaluation (and, of course, student assessment). This, however, is a weak and watered-down form of judgement, hardly worthy of the title. When we ask our students critically to assess an argument or research report, we expect them to follow a particular formula, strategy or method and to arrive at the correct or accepted conclusion, whether by applying the criteria for valid empirical research or the dialectical method for synthesizing a conclusion from a series of diverse or contradictory statements. I was a particularly slow learner in this regard. I recall during my second year as an undergraduate thinking that an essay title asking me to critique Descartes' ontological argument for the existence of God was, in fact, asking me to critique Descartes' ontological argument for the existence of God; that is to say, it was asking *me* to critique it rather than to assemble (from the Latin *simul* together) the critiques of other writers (that is, to produce a *simulation* of a critique). Fortunately, I learnt the language and vocabulary of the student essay title just in time for my final exams.

We are, in most cases, not asking our students to make a judgement but rather for the *simulation* of a judgement. As Lyotard points out, 'judgement' is the name of a language game that cannot be reduced to a list of rules and procedures. The only judgement worthy of the title is the 'enigmatic' judgement, 'the one which follows no rules'[63] and which cannot be explicated in terms of other language games. When I read a student assignment and 'just know' that it is (say) a 'good 2.2', I am making a judgment. When I complete a marking grid and award a score for each section to arrive at a final aggregated mark, I am *simulating* a judgement. The problem with which I am increasingly faced as an intuitive marker is that I am being called more and more to offer a rationale for my professional, intuitive, experienced-based 'enigmatic' judgement, and I find that I am unable explicitly to account for myself in an articulate, logical way to the satisfaction of exam boards and quality control committees.[64] And so, in the absence of accountability, I am forced to turn to accountancy.

(The argument against intuitive expert marking based on many years of experience is that not all markers have the necessary experience to draw upon, and so equity cannot be guaranteed. Thus, if novices are unable to mark in the same way as experts, we must all mark like novices. The only exception appears to be in the case of external examiners, where experience, expertise and a global perspective are seen as positive qualities, and where judgements from examiners beginning with the phrase 'In my experience...' are still welcomed.)

If 'judgement' is a contested term when thinking about the essay, then so too is 'writing'. If I am to understand what is meant by 'writing an essay', then I need to explore further the *very idea(s)* of 'writing', both as a verb and a noun. I should begin, I suppose, by stating the obvious: in semiological terms, the *idea* of a word (the signified) is related to the verbal or written form of the word (the signifier) only contingently. (That is to say, there is no logical relationship between the word 'writing' and the idea of writing.) Similarly, the form and the idea together (the sign) has only a contingent relationship to its referent 'out there' in the world. We derive the meanings of words not by their association to something 'out there', but in relation to other words. Thus, I understand the meaning of the word and the concept 'writing' by recognizing its differences from the words and concepts 'drawing' or 'speaking'.[65] An understanding of how writing is distinguished from drawing, speaking and other forms of communication and expression is therefore fundamental to recognizing what it means to write.

We know that writing emerged from drawing, and that the first written symbols in most scripts, including Chinese, Egyptian and Greek/Latin, were pictographs and ideograms; writing is (or, at least, was) a form of drawing. However, the nature of the relationship between writing and speaking is more complex and contested. It is widely accepted that writing was developed initially as a form of accountancy or record-keeping, possibly by farmers as a way of keeping track of their livestock; that is, as an *aide memoire*. For this reason, writing is usually regarded as supplementary to speech, as an afterthought and an addendum. Speech is immediate and immanent, writing is merely a system developed in order to represent and record the spoken word (Voltaire referred to it as 'voice-painting'); speech denotes presence, writing emphasizes the absence of the speaker; speech is fluid, responsive and alive; writing is rigid, fixed and dead.

Derrida traces this view of writing from the Egyptian myth of Thoth, god of writing (as recounted by Plato in the *Phaedrus*), through to nineteenth- and twentieth-century accounts by Rousseau, Saussure and Levi-Strauss.[66] In a series of essays,[67] Derrida attempts to deconstruct this supplementary relationship, where writing emerged as nothing more than a device for recording the spoken word, and suggests instead that speech and writing developed separately from the same 'trace', which he describes as the common root of speech *and* writing and which he refers to as *arche-writing*. Barthes expresses the fundamental separation of speaking and writing another way. Teaching is rooted in the Greek idea of rhetoric (from *rhētōr*, orator), and teachers are therefore 'on the side of speech'. Intellectuals are those teachers who 'write up' and publish their speeches and are thus also on the side of speech. However, 'the writer stands apart, separate. Writing begins at the point where speech becomes *impossible*'.[68]

Once prised away from its supplementary relationship to speech, writing (and hence the essay) can begin to take on a character and a function of its own. Clearly, writing still retains its recording function (personified by Barthes's intellectual), which can be seen in the transcript, the write-up and the textbook. However, once writing breaks free of its mimetic obligation, its *inaugural* nature is revealed. Derrida suggests that writing serves a *revelatory* function by uncovering what is hidden from us. [69] Thus, he cites Husserl: 'My own words take me by surprise and teach me what I think'; that is to say, as I write I discover what I already know. Writing, then, is *dangerous* and *anguishing* since it does not know where it is going.[70] Picking up a pen and 'just writing' is rather like opening my mouth and just talking (but as we have seen quite different from transcribing my speech). When I start a sentence (whether spoken or written) I often have no clear idea in my mind where and how it might end, and I often surprise myself. In this sense, writing (in the idiomatic form of 'writing an essay') does not reproduce, it creates.

It is in this sense of 'just writing' that Roland Barthes has raised the question of whether the verb *to write* can have an intransitive form (that is, a verb without a direct object); whether it is possible simply to write, as he says, *absolutely*.[71] If this is indeed the case, and if 'writing an essay' is simply an expression of the intransitive verb *to write*, then it is apparent that the noun 'essay' does not name anything, but is simply an indication that I am referring to a particular activity called 'writing absolutely' or 'just writing'. Writing an essay is therefore an activity of a very different order from writing a report or even from writing a book: books and reports are written in order to be read; essays are just written, that is, their purpose is in the writing itself. If I say that I am writing a book, I am stating *what* I am writing. If I say that I am writing an essay, I am stating *how* I am writing. This in turn begs the question: *What is it that I am writing when I am writing an essay (that is, when I am 'just writing')?* To the extent that such a question can have a meaningful answer, Roland Barthes provides a clue: 'I am writing a text and I call it R.B.',[72] or, if I may be permitted: I am writing an essay and I call it G.R.

When I write an essay I am composing myself, that is, I am writing largely out of my own subconscious. Many of us are familiar with this experience of 'just writing', of waiting expectantly to find out just what it is that we think about a particular issue, and of sometimes being surprised at what appears on the page in front of us. My advice to colleagues and students who are struggling with a writing assignment is, invariably, 'just write', and many other writers and authors, far more accomplished than me, have remarked in wonder at how words and sentences often appear out of nowhere, as if by magic. The novelist and critic Hélène Cixous marvels that 'this page writes itself without help, it is the proof of the existence of gods',[73] a feeling echoed by the writer and poet Edmond Jabès in his advice that 'The art of the writer consists in, little by little, making words interest themselves in his books'.[74] I can, of course, only write what I already know, but as Jabès points out elsewhere: 'You do not write what you know, but what you are unaware you know and then discover, without surprise, you have always known.'[75]

When I claim that writing an essay is 'just writing', I am, of course, playing on both meanings of the word 'just'. Just *writing* is writing for the sake of writing, where the point is not to create a text to be read but simply to discover what I already know. But *just* writing is also the process of writing a *judgement* (from the Latin *jus* – right) and thus of reintroducing the *question of value* back into the heart of university life. When I write an essay, I am discovering what I think about a particular issue, and I justify my opinions by drawing on my own experience, ideas and values; that is to say, I am attempting to replace monetary value with what Readings calls 'the question of evaluation' as the legitimating idea of the university. As Lyotard tells us, 'In every instance, one must evaluate relations: of force, of values, of qualities and of quantities; but to evaluate them there are no criteria, nothing but opinions.'[76] In the corporate University of Excellence, where adherence to Method is the guarantor of truth, certainty and marketable information, writing an essay is the final act of subversion and the last best hope for judgement, critique and independent thought.

I have suggested in this book that the subversive mission of the paraversity is to build (in Heidegger's meaning of the word) a community of thought dedicated to dissensus; to raise questions of significance, importance and value to academic life and to resist all attempts to reduce them to a single 'right' answer through imposed consensual agreement. To think and to write in parallel; students, lecturers and researchers together; 'beside each other and beside ourselves',[77] is not to reject the idea and the practice of judgement in favour of a simple agreement to disagree. On the contrary, it means placing value judgements at the very core of what it means to work and study in a university. As Readings warns, 'Those in the University are called upon to judge, and the administration will do it for them if they do not respond to the call.'[78] If we wish to resist Readings' vision of the corporate university as 'a bureaucratic apparatus for the production, distribution, and consumption of knowledge',[79] then we must surely begin by reasserting the practice of 'just writing' as the primary means through which the university talks to itself and to the outside world.

Chapter 7

On the seminar

'Is this a real site or an imaginary one? Neither. An institution is treated in the utopian mode: I outline a space and call it: *seminar*'.

Roland Barthes, *To the Seminar*, 1974

The question of teaching

It is only comparatively recently that the university began to define itself in relation to teaching. We have seen already that Humboldt's blueprint for the modern university had at its heart the activity of *learning* rather than teaching or research. That is not to say that teaching had no place in Humboldt's university, but rather, as Lewis Elton has pointed out, that teaching has traditionally been framed in terms of the advancement of knowledge through learning and research rather than as a method of instruction, and the primary concern of the academic has always been to learn rather than to teach.[1] For Humboldt, then, 'the teacher does not exist for the sake of the student; both teacher and student have their justification in the *common pursuit of knowledge*'.[2] When Humboldt describes teaching in these terms, he is suggesting that, if not the *only* way of pursuing knowledge, the practice of teaching is certainly the most effective way. Thus 'the teacher's performance depends on the student's presence and interest – without this, science and scholarship [*Wissenschaft*] could not grow'.[3] Learning, scholarship and the advancement of knowledge therefore require what Humboldt terms a 'synthesis of the teacher's and the student's dispositions', to the extent that 'If the students who are to form his audience did not come before him of their own free will, he, in his quest for knowledge, would have to seek them out.'[4] That is not to say that the teacher–student relationship is an equal partnership, or that each party makes an equal contribution to it. Perhaps the paradigm case of this 'synthesis of dispositions' is Wittgenstein's method of teaching from a deckchair at Cambridge during the 1930s. In a 'biographical sketch', Anthony Kenny describes it thus:

Wittgenstein sat in his deckchair, in flannels, a leather jacket and an open-necked shirt. He used no manuscript or notes, but wrestled aloud with philosophical problems, interrupting his exposition with long silences and passionate questioning of his audience.[5]

We can only speculate what modern-day students might have made of this, and of how they would have rated Wittgenstein in the National Student Survey, and yet we know from the responses of some of those who were present that something both extraordinary and creative was occurring; something that manuscripts or notes would surely have stifled.

As we can see from this account, the idea of the university as a site where academics and students pursued learning side by side persisted well into the twentieth century. Oakeshott, writing in 1950, identified the 'distinctive mark of a university' as 'a place where [the student] has the opportunity of education in conversation with his teachers, his fellows and himself',[6] and as late as 1969 F.R. Leavis described teaching in terms of a collaboration between academics and students at all levels, even with 'first- or second-year men' (sic). Thus, the teacher

> tests and develops in 'teaching' his perceptions, his understanding and his thought, and with good men [students] may do so very fruitfully. For what we call teaching is, if genuine, a matter of enlisting and fostering collaboration . . . [7]

However, he continues, 'I see the word "teaching" in inverted commas. I don't like it, because of the suggestion it carries of telling – authoritative telling'.[8]

If we are to understand better what it means to teach, then it is important that we distinguish between at least two uses of the word. Lewis Elton notes that 'Teaching is . . . one of the few verbs in the English language that has two objects – one teaches students a subject.'[9] When Leavis describes 'genuine' teaching as enlisting and fostering the collaboration of his students, he is referring to *teaching students*; that is, to engaging with others in the pursuit of learning. When he places the term in inverted commas because of its connotation of authoritative telling, he is referring to *teaching a subject*. As Maskell and Robinson add:

> . . . what does it mean to teach *Macbeth* or *The Rainbow*, if not to give students a, or even the, correct way of taking a book? And what is that but, one way or another, the replacement of thought by indoctrination? Or of something yet lower down the intellectual scale, the mere repetition of a tutor's notes?[10]

To teach students is to engage with them in the pursuit of learning, whilst to teach a subject is more likely to entail the transmission of existing knowledge and information. In order to distinguish between these two meanings, I will refer here to Leavis's 'teaching' (in inverted commas) as the lecture (from the Latin *lectus* to read), which typically involves the teacher reading from a book or set of notes, or nowadays from PowerPoint slides; and to his 'genuine' teaching as the seminar (from the Latin *seminarium* – seed bed, which is conceptually related to *educare* – to rear or to grow). In making this distinction, I am referring neither to specific teaching methods nor to seating arrangements, but rather to attitudes and relationships; what Oakeshott would have called 'manners'. Whereas the lecture establishes a didactic relationship and adopts a denotative mode of address, the seminar is dialogic, discursive and open-ended. It is, however, just as possible (perhaps more so) to indoctrinate students in small groups through so-called person-centred methods as it is in the lecture theatre. Conversely, I have had first-hand experience of productive discussion and debate in a tiered lecture hall surrounded by several hundred other students. The manners of teaching transcend physical and structural boundaries and can be brought to bear on any student–teacher interaction.

The lecture

Perhaps unsurprisingly, the lecture is rapidly becoming the teaching method of choice in the corporate university, where time is of the essence and the communication of the information required to pass examinations has come to replace learning and scholarship in importance. However, whilst the lecture is an appropriate way of conducting the business transaction of exchanging information and qualifications for cash and high ratings in the National Student Survey, it has very little to contribute to the process of education. In a very relevant analogy for the current times, Paulo Freire referred in 1972 to the 'banking' concept of education, where lecturing

> becomes an act of depositing, in which the students are the depositories and the teacher is the depositor. Instead of communicating, the teacher issues communiqués and 'makes deposits' which the students patiently receive, memorize, and repeat.[11]

As we might imagine, the lecture not only reduces the students to 'patient, listening objects' and 'receptacles to be filled by the teacher', but also renders the subject matter 'motionless, static, compartmentalized, predictable'. In anticipation of the current results-driven, performance-indicator-led culture, Freire observes that 'the more completely [the lecturer] fills the receptacles, the better a teacher he is. The more meekly the receptacles permit themselves to be filled, the better students they are'.[12] 'Good' students do not disrupt the efficient flow of information with questions or challenges, a lesson that most of them quickly learn from their fellow students rather than from their lecturers.

Just as the lecturer 'presents himself to his students as their necessary opposite',[13] so lecturing is presented as the necessary opposite of learning. Lecturing is the active process of filling with knowledge; learning is the passive process of being filled. Lecturing is the process of externalizing and transmitting the lecturer's knowledge; learning is the process through which the student receives and internalizes it. Furthermore, knowledge is 'static': the success of lecturing is measured by the extent to which the knowledge transmitted by the lecturer is received unchanged and undistorted by the student and later accurately reproduced in essays and examinations. According to this 'banking' account of teaching and learning, learning is a purely internal psychological process. As such it is individual and solitary: to learn is to commit to memory, and the concept of 'learning together' makes no more sense than that of dreaming together. Thus, the Enlightenment idea of the university as a community of learners is called into question; learning in the corporate University of Excellence does not depend on the company of other learners, nor even on the presence of a teacher. There is, of course, a certain irony at work here, insofar as the kind of learning that is delivered through the lecture is probably more efficiently achieved in the library or in front of a computer screen without the presence or the need of a lecturer. That is to say, what the lecture does best is better done through other means. As Carl Rogers observes, 'Why the lecture is regarded as a major means of instruction is a mystery. It made sense before books were published, but its current rationale is almost never explained.'[14]

It is perhaps partly from a tacit acknowledgement that the physical presence of lecturers, fellow students and even the university campus are unnecessary for the kind of learning demanded by students and offered by the corporate university, that attention has recently turned away from education towards the wider 'student experience'. For example, the strategic plan for my university talks of 'student life-cycle development work' and 'an associated student relationship management system' and aspires 'to remain "high touch" retaining the breadth of face to face service provision, whilst becoming more "high tech" with increased self-access information, advice and guidance'.[15] I am not entirely sure what any of this means, but I suspect that it relates to the realization that, if learning amounts to little more than sitting in a room on a campus absorbing facts directly from a laptop screen, then the room, the campus and the wider non-academic social experiences on offer take on a greater significance in attracting students to particular universities, and in ensuring their satisfaction when they arrive.

From the point of view of the corporate university, then, the terms 'teaching' and 'learning' are used primarily to describe the transmission and reception of facts from lecturer to student. Furthermore, despite the claim that lecturing is the mirror image or 'necessary opposite' of learning, even the briefest consideration will reveal that this is, in fact, far from being the case. On the one hand, learning of the kind described above does not require a lecturer; on the other hand, attending a lecture is no guarantee that learning has taken place. Learning and teaching, in the guise of lecturing and memorizing, are two separate and independent activities, neither of which entails the other. The reciprocal process to 'teaching' is, by this account, not 'learning' but 'being taught'.[16] This realization that the university is no longer necessary or even required for the learning of facts in order to pass examinations perhaps accounts for the absence of any mention of learning or education in the mission statement of my university, to be replaced with the new corporate mission of producing graduates. If the corporate university has less and less influence over student learning, then at least it still has a monopoly on the awarding of degrees.

The return to education

In the face of a corporate university mission that has replaced the shared pursuit of learning with the assembly-line production of graduates, the role and responsibility of the paraversity is twofold: first to reintegrate the work of the teacher as necessary to the process of learning; and second to promote and facilitate a view of learning that moves it beyond the memorization and regurgitation of information and facts. That is to say, the subversive mission of the paraversity is to reinstate education as its central activity and purpose.

The return to education is a return to a social model of teaching and learning that regards them as more than simply a mechanical process for the transmission of information. For Oakeshott, education is a 'human engagement' and a 'transaction between the generations' that involves 'learning to perform humanly'. He continues:

> Education is not acquiring a stock of ready-made ideas, images, sentiments, beliefs and so forth; it is learning to look, to listen, to think, to feel, to imagine, to believe, to understand, to choose and to wish.[17]

We can perhaps see already why this mission to reinstate education at the heart of university life is not only likely to produce a subversive and disruptive effect, but also why it must be conducted in a subversive and surreptitious manner. We must assume that neither the corporate university nor its students will necessarily recognize the value of learning to imagine, to believe and to wish as instrumental or important in the production of graduates *per se*, and the teaching necessary to stimulate such learning must therefore be undertaken surreptitiously and in parallel to the teaching of facts and information.

If Oakeshott's idea of education was fundamentally different from the corporate mission of learning as the internalization of facts, then it would be difficult to imagine how the subversive teacher might accomplish both tasks in parallel. Fortunately, however, Oakeshott regards education primarily as the acquisition of knowledge, where knowledge is *information plus judgement*. In other words, the educational enterprise *includes* the mission of the corporate university in the form of the transmission of information, but adds to it the development of judgement.[18] Oakeshott's idea of information corresponds more or less to Freire's banking concept. For Oakeshott, information

> is the explicit ingredient of knowledge, where what we know may be itemized. Information consists of facts, specific intellectual artifacts (often arranged in sets or bunches). It is impersonal (not a matter of opinion). Most of it is accepted on authority, and it is to be found in dictionaries, manuals, textbooks and encyclopedias.[19]

Philosophers often refer to this as 'propositional knowledge' because it can be expressed in the form of verbal statements.

If this was all that knowledge consisted of, then education would indeed be simply a matter of making a deposit in the students' memory banks, or even, as Oakeshott appears to suggest, of pointing them in the direction of the sources of this information so that they could make their own deposit. However, information is only one ingredient of knowledge, the other of which is judgement. Oakeshott continues:

> By 'judgement' I mean the tacit or implicit component of knowledge, the ingredient which is not merely unspecified in propositions but is unspecifiable in propositions. It is the component of knowledge which does not appear in the form of rules and which, therefore, cannot be resolved into information or itemized in the manner characteristic of information.[20]

Oakeshott is at pains to point out that judgement is not simply another kind of information, but is something of a completely different order, related to Gilbert Ryle's concepts of 'knowing that' and 'knowing how'. Furthermore, whilst we usually think of judgement in relation to 'manual and sensual skills', Oakeshott believes that its role in intellectual activities such as art, literature, historical, philosophical and scientific understanding is 'almost immeasurably greater'.[21] Judgement, then, 'is being able to think...with an appreciation of the considerations which belong to different modes of thought'.[22] To judge is to think reflexively, to think about thinking, and corresponds more or less to what Readings referred to as 'the name of Thought'.[23]

Knowledge is therefore made up of two separate and quite distinct components, the propositional and the tacit; that which can be expressed clearly and unambiguously and that which cannot. The next question for Oakeshott is thus: 'What bearing has this view of things upon the activities of learning and teaching?'[24] His response is that the two components of knowledge can both be communicated by the teacher and can both be acquired by the learner. However, they cannot be taught and learnt separately (either on separate occasions or in separate lessons) and they cannot be taught and learnt in the same way. Thus, for Oakeshott, teaching is a 'twofold activity' of communicating information (instructing) and communicating judgement (imparting). Judgement 'cannot be taught separately; it can have no place of its own in a timetable or curriculum...but it may be taught in everything that is taught'. Learning is, similarly, a twofold activity of acquiring information and coming to possess judgement, and once again, judgement 'cannot be learned separately...but it may be learned in everything that is learned'.[25] In response to Maskell and Robinson's little 'catch' that 'Thought can't be taught',[26] Oakeshott would probably have wished to add the words 'by and of itself'.

This analysis of learning and teaching suggests that lecturing is inadequate as a means to education, for whilst the lecture might be employed to communicate information, it is not a particularly good method for imparting judgement. Similarly, whilst information can be acquired and memorized solely from books and databases, judgement (that is the ability to think) can never be imparted in this way. As Alasdair MacIntyre observes, 'It is a familiar truth that one can only think for oneself if one does not think by oneself.'[27] Thus, whilst lectures, books and on-line sources of information might be adequate learning and teaching strategies for passing assignments and examinations, they do not provide the student with an education. To become educated – in the sense that I have used the term in this book – the student must learn to make judgements, that is to think critically. As we have seen, Oakeshott believes that this learning can only occur in conjunction with the learning of facts and information but that it is taught and learnt in a quite different way. On the one hand, judgement 'is implanted [in the student] unobtrusively in the manner in which information is conveyed, in a tone of voice, in the gesture which accompanies instruction, in asides and oblique utterances, and by example'.[28] It can, to some extent, be imparted simply by 'overhearing an intelligent conversation',[29] perhaps between a lecturer and another student, or even between two students.

However, the practice of judgement also requires an *active* participation in the process, which is best achieved through what Freire describes as 'problem-posing education'.[30] The problem-posing method is not merely a technique or a strategy for teaching; it reconfigures the relationship between the teacher and the student from didactic to dialogic,[31] and thus addresses the 'manners' of teaching and learning. Thus,

> the problem-posing method – *dialogical par excellence* – is constituted and organised by the student's view of the world...The task of the dialogical teacher...is to 're-present' [the world view of the students]...and 're-present' it not as a lecture, but as a problem.[32]

Bill Readings also advocates dialogism as an approach to teaching, although his view is closer to the 'pure' form outlined by Bakhtin. Readings points out that dialogism is not simply 'the capacity for reversed or serial monologue',[33] that is to say, it should not be understood merely as opening a space for dialogue. It is, rather, the recognition (predominantly on the part of the teacher) that communication is never a simple verbal transaction and that the transfer of meaning can never be guaranteed. To enter into a dialogical relationship is to acknowledge that the person with whom we are engaging in discourse is never an empty vessel and that 'what a sender [of a message] says takes its place amid a crowd of idiolects in the listener, and their conversation acquires its sense in a discursive act of which neither is the master'.[34] Readings continues: 'teaching, then, is not primarily a matter of communication between autonomous subjects functioning alternately as senders and receivers',[35] but is rather 'a *relation, a network of obligation*'.[36]

When Oakeshott identifies judgement as an essential component of knowledge, he is referring to a process rather than an outcome, to a verb rather than a noun. The aim of education is not to arrive at a predetermined final judgement in the form of a Hegelian dialectical synthesis of thesis and antithesis; that is to say, it is not to anticipate the 'correct' answers to textbook problems. The purpose of education is not to teach *judgements* (that is, previously arrived-at accepted views or *doxa*), but *judgement*, the practice of being able to think through problems for ourselves and to arrive at our own solutions. Education, then, is not merely the *transmission* of thought from teacher to student (although it will, of course, contain an element of this), but the *production* of thought, where the role of the teacher is (to use Oakeshott's terminology) not to instruct but to impart.

The development of the facility of judgement is not something that can be achieved alone; it requires the company and participation of others. Judgement is developed by trying it out, by practising it and by listening to other people attempting to do the same. The development of judgement requires a community of critical friends committed to the process of thinking together, not in order to arrive at consensus but, on the contrary, to keep debate open and Thought (that is, Readings' 'name of Thought') in circulation. Whilst it is possible to achieve this with classes of all sizes and in rooms of all shapes (including lecture theatres), it demands particular attitudes, skills and commitments from all the participants.

The topology of the seminar

It will be recalled from earlier that I proposed the seminar (the seed bed) as a more appropriate alternative to the lecture for the paraversity. I made the point that, in using the term 'seminar', I was referring neither to specific teaching methods nor to class size or seating arrangements, adding that the seminar is concerned more with manners than with method. I was influenced in my choice of terminology by Roland Barthes's short paper *To the Seminar*, first published in 1974, which 'outlines a space' that is neither real nor imaginary, but should be thought of as 'utopian'.[37] Barthes further develops his outline of the space of the seminar by describing a 'subtle topology of corporeal relations', which includes three spaces and three educational practices.

The three spaces of the seminar

The first space of the seminar is *institutional*. Barthes suggests that the institution determines a frequency, a schedule, a site and sometimes a *cursus* (a course of study). However, Barthes insists that the institution does not and cannot impose a hierarchy on the seminar, either of participants or of knowledge. That is to say, all participants are accorded equal respect and all knowledge claims are given an equal hearing; there is no attempt to defer to a hierarchy of knowledge and thereby to close down debate. We might say, *pace* Deleuze, that the institutional space of the seminar is rhizomatic rather than arborescent; horizontal and inclusive rather than vertical and stratified.

The second space of the seminar is *transferential* insofar as it is concerned with relationships. Barthes identifies two classes of relationships within the seminar: those between the director and its members (his terms) and the 'horizontal transferences' of the members to each other. He suggests that the members initially look to the director as a source of authority in both senses of the word, but that the role of the director is to provide neither. On the one hand, the director is not present in the traditional authoritative role of the professor: 'I am not draped in the interminable discourse of absolute knowledge, I am not lurking in the terrifying silence of the Examiner.' Neither does the director supply a store of authoritative information: 'I do not say what I know, I set forth what I am doing.' Rather than deliver a lecture, the role of the director is 'to clear the stage on which horizontal transferences will be established', that is, to open up a space for communication between the seminar members. As such, the director is 'a regulator: the one who gives rules, protocols, not laws'.[38]

The third space of the seminar is *textual*. Barthes is suitably vague in his description of this space, but he would appear to be using the term 'textual' in a wider sense than simply to refer to a written output. Thus he makes reference to 'the rarest text, one which does not appear in writing' and to 'texts which are not products but practices'.[39] It is likely that he is drawing here on his earlier distinction between the teacher 'who is on the side of speech' and the writer, 'every operator of language on the side of writing'.[40] This attempt to distance the textual nature of the seminar from the oral approach of lecturing – 'writing begins at the point where speech becomes *impossible*'[41] – will become more apparent when we go on to consider Barthes's practices of the seminar.

The three spaces of the seminar are presented as an integrated whole:

'none is judged (disparaged, praised), none prevails over its neighbors'.[42] Each is the supplement of the other two and the work of the seminar is 'the *production of differences*'.[43] However, difference is not regarded as conflict but as the discovery of originality. We might say, then, with Readings, that the seminar offers a space for dissensus, 'where thought takes place beside thought, where thinking is a shared process without identity or unity'.[44]

Three educational practices

Barthes asks us to imagine (or perhaps to remember) three educational practices. The first is *teaching*, in which 'a (previous) knowledge is transmitted by oral or written discourse, swathed in a flux of statements (books, manuals, lectures)'.[45] This description is more or less identical to Leavis's 'teaching' (in inverted commas), which I have referred to in this chapter as lecturing. The second is *apprenticeship*, where 'the "master" ... works *for himself* in the apprentice's presence'.[46] The example given earlier of Wittgenstein teaching from his deckchair is perhaps the paradigm case of the apprenticeship as an educational practice. The master wrestles with a problem and the apprentice is introduced to the process by which the problem is resolved. What is learnt is not the solution to *this* problem, but the (general) solution to problems *of this type*. Another example would be Oakeshott's reflection from his own education of the importance of 'those occasions when one was not being talked to but had the opportunity of overhearing an intelligent conversation'.[47]

Barthes's third educational practice is *mothering*, which he describes in the following way:

> When a child learns to walk, the mother neither speaks nor demonstrates; she does not teach walking, she does not represent it (she does not walk before the child): she supports, encourages, calls (steps back and calls); she incites and surrounds: the child demands the mother and the mother desires the child's walking ...[48]

The educational practice of mothering is a poetic and emotive articulation of what Carl Rogers had previously referred to as student-centred learning, which draws on the innate biological and psychological drive of the student towards self-actualization. Rogers regards the educator as a 'facilitator of learning', whose role is primarily to provide a permissive and nurturing environment in which the student can flourish and grow without any direct instruction. Thus 'the facilitator relies on the desire of each student to implement those purposes that have meaning for him or her as the motivational force behind significant learning'.[49] Other notable advocates of Barthes's 'mothering' approach to education include Malcolm Knowles, who focuses specifically on the adult learner and who argues that adults are driven by a 'need to know';[50] and Paulo Freire, who believes that 'men [are] beings in the process of *becoming*' and 'in this incompleteness and this awareness lie the very roots of education as an exclusively human manifestation'.[51] In each of these examples, the process of education is driven by the students' desire to learn and the educators' desire to see them learn. The educator, like the mother, does not teach but simply allows learning to happen. As Carl Rogers famously said, 'Teaching is, for me, a relatively unimportant and vastly over-rated activity';[52] that is to say, learning (whether learning to walk or learning to reason) would occur regardless of the educator, whose role is to create the optimum environment for human flourishing.

For Barthes, the director of the seminar rejects the practice of teaching in favour of the apprenticeship and mothering. Thus:

> In the seminar (and this is its definition), all teaching is foreclosed: no knowledge is transmitted (but a knowledge can be created), no discourse is sustained (but a text is sought): teaching is *disappointed*.[53]

The seminar is therefore defined very broadly, not by what is included, but by what is proscribed or 'disappointed'. Regarded in this way, the seminar is, by definition, the very opposite of the lecture.

Conclusion: teaching and learning in the paraversity

The aim of the paraversity is to subvert the mission of the corporate University of Excellence, and one of the most important and effective ways through which this might be achieved is by reasserting the importance of learning. I remain incredulous to the fact that my university can proudly advocate a mission that mentions neither learning nor education, and has replaced them with 'an associated student relationship management system'. I can only speculate that learning no longer features as part of the university mission because the university has recognized that it has very little to contribute to the kind of learning that it is promoting and which students are demanding, beyond providing access to the internet and a reasonably stocked library. And we should not forget that, until relatively recently, learn-ing was considered to be the primary activity not only of students, but also of academics, and that education was promoted as the common pursuit of knowledge *by all* through mutual talking and listening.

However, the purpose of the paraversity is not only to *reinstate* learning but to *reintegrate* it with teaching. I have suggested that the lecture (the activity that provides many academics with their job titles) has contributed to a separation of learning and teaching, to the extent that neither is dependent on the other. A great deal of what is now learnt in the modern university does not come from attending lectures and, I would suggest, many lectures do not result in very much (if any) learning. To reintegrate teaching and learning is to find a way to reconfigure them as reciprocal practices – indeed, as two aspects of the *same* practice.

Such a reconfiguration can be achieved in a number of ways through a number of teaching strategies. The aim of this chapter has not been to outline particular practices or techniques, but rather to address the broader issue of manners; that is, of the relationships and structures necessary for students and academics to begin to talk to each other in the common pursuit of learning. This in turn demands that we think again about the kinds of knowledge that the university ought to be concerned with, and hence the kinds of learning appropriate to that knowledge. I have suggested, with Michael Oakeshott, that the most important component of knowledge is the ability to make judgements, and that learning to make judgements is best done through observation and conversation. Learning is therefore a social activity, a joint enterprise whose purpose is not to transmit knowledge from one brain to another, but actively to create it through a co-operative and collegiate partnership.

Chapter 8

On the book

'I was shocked at college to see one hundred of my classmates in the library all reading copies of the same book. Instead of doing as they did, I went into the stacks and read the first book written by an author whose name began with Z. I received the highest grade in the class. That convinced me that the institution was not being run correctly. I left.'

John Cage, *An Autobiographical Statement*, 1988

Rebuilding the library

Stefan Collini, Professor of Intellectual History and English Literature at Cambridge University, relates the story of a newly appointed vice chancellor who requested to come and see him at work on his research. Collini tells how he brooded over exactly what 'carrying on with my research' might mean, and what the vice chancellor might be expecting to witness as he entered Collini's office:

> Should I be correcting the proofs of my latest publication, or be discussing my exciting new 'findings' with one of my colleagues, or be on the point of filling in a large grant application? Finally, I realized that if I was supposed to represent 'research in the humanities' it was clear what I ought to be doing: I ought to be sitting alone reading a book.[1]

'Reading a book' has, until recent times, been the defining feature of what it means to be an academic, not only in the humanities, but across the entire university. If the definition of a university is, as Bill Readings suggests, a disparate group of people united by a common complaint about parking, then it is also a collection of buildings constructed around a library. Doctoral students might write their theses, but undergraduates *read* for a degree, and that has, until recently, meant sitting in a library surrounded by books.

It might reasonably be claimed, therefore, that the primary defining feature, the icon of the Enlightenment university, is the book. Whilst the idea of a university without a philosophy department is no longer unthinkable, the idea of a university without a library remains so, at least for now. The book is the (quite literal) embodiment of learning and reason, and the most powerful way of symbolizing the rejection of reason, scholarship and civilized debate is the burning of books. I am not talking here about the *concept* or the *idea* of the book, but of *books*, of the objects that can (or should) be found on the shelves of every scholar, every student. Books are the repository of knowledge and libraries are the repositories of books. To paraphrase Collini, books have traditionally been regarded as essential to the maintenance, extension and transmission of intellectual enquiry,[2] although in the University of Excellence they are coming to be valued more and more simply as receptacles of information and facts, hence John Cage's dismay at finding one hundred of his fellow students all sitting in the library reading copies of the same book.[3] If we are to construct the paraversity in the ruins of the Enlightenment university, the library is the place to begin laying the (metaphorical) foundations.

In this final chapter, I return to the format employed in Chapter 6 and offer two essays on the book. In the first, entitled *What is a book?*, I explore the distinction between the book as a receptacle for information and as a vehicle for intellectual enquiry. Drawing predominantly on the work of Gilles Deleuze and Roland Barthes, I suggest that this distinction is not simply a matter of content, but of how that content is organized and presented, and how the reader approaches it. If we return for a moment to Cage's example of one hundred students all reading the same book, I might argue, along with Barthes, that in certain cases it would be conceptually impossible for even two people to read the same book, just as it would be impossible for the same person to read the same book twice (not least because, on the second reading, the person would no longer be the same – and neither would the book). Collini's association of being an academic with reading a book therefore hinges as much on the questions What kind of reader? and What kind of reading? as on What kind of book?

The second and final essay is a little gift to myself as a reward for completing this book. I first came across the short stories of the Argentinean writer Jorge Luis Borges as a student in the 1970s, and I have been fascinated ever since by the philosophical questions he manages to raise and speculate upon through such a concise and unlikely medium. One story in particular caught my imagination, and I have returned to it again and again over the past 40 years. In *The Library of Babel* Borges tells of a 'total library' that contains not only every book ever written, but every book that *could* ever be written, and imagines some of the epistemological and existential consequences of having the totality of all possible knowledge at our disposal, and being unable to distinguish between what of it is true and what is fabricated.[4] In my essay, which quotes extensively from Borges's work, I expand on the theme of imaginary books and speculate on the dissolving boundaries between the real, the fictional and the fictitious. Neither of these essays sets out to provide answers, but only to raise further questions. The chapter concludes, fittingly, with a last word from Bill Readings, followed by a final word from Jacques Derrida.

First attempt: what is a book?

> **book** *noun* **1** a set of written, printed, lined or blank sheets bound together. **2** a long written or printed composition. [Old English *bōc* beech tree]

The machine book

Perhaps the most concise answer to the question What is a book? is provided by Gilles Deleuze and Félix Guattari, who describe it simply as 'a little machine'.[5] As we saw in Chapter 3, Deleuze and Guattari define a machine as a node or a component in a larger assemblage; thus, machines temporarily 'plug in' to one another to form networks and structures for the performance of particular tasks. Machines take their meanings from the assemblage they are currently plugged into and the task for which that assemblage was constructed. To ask What a book *is*, is therefore, to ask What it is *for*. Thus:

> We will never ask what a book means, as signified or signifier; we will not look for anything to understand in it. We will ask what it functions with, in connection with what other things . . . when one writes, the only question is which other machine the literary machine can be plugged into, must be plugged into in order to work.[6]

A book is a little machine; we judge a book not by its cover but by what it does and with whom it associates. Books might usefully be regarded as machines that regulate flow: a book regulates the flow of words, of sentences, of ideas; a book stops and starts the flow, it dissects and orders it into parts, into chapters; the book machine plugs into other machines, including other books and members of the academic community. When academics, students or administrators form an assemblage with one or more books they become readers, writers, researchers, librarians and so on. Books are therefore not defined by a hard cover or by a certain number of pages, not by genre or subject matter; a book is simply a machine that regulates the flow of energy; it stimulates and stems the flow of thoughts and ideas.

Deleuze and Guattari identify two types of book. The root-book represents the classical idea of the book and of thought, and takes as its image the tree (perhaps, as the etymologists tell us, the *bōc*, the beech tree), 'with its pivotal spine and surrounding leaves';[7] a central core, rooted in the earth, in the world, supporting a structured and ordered array of branches and leaves.

'The tree articulates and hierarchizes tracings; tracings are like the leaves of a tree.'[8] The root-book imposes what classical thought takes to be a natural order, the order of nature, on the flow of energy and ideas, which it directs from root to branch, from branch to root, along a certain predetermined route. The root-/route-book imagines that it mirrors the world in both its content and its structure, and therefore carries and encourages the expectation that it will tell or explain what the world is like. However, Deleuze and Guattari caution that 'contrary to deep rooted belief, the book is not an image of the world. It forms a rhizome with the world...',[9] that is, it enters into a partnership with people and with other books. All attempts by the classic root-book to produce a tracing (that is a faithful reproduction) of the world will inevitably end in disappointment.

The second type of book, then, is the rhizomatic book, whose image is the tuber or the rhizome. Whereas the tree-like root-book is linear and hierarchical in form and structure with a beginning, a middle and an end (in that order), the tuberous rhizomatic book is a decentred, subterranean network in which all points are connected to all others. A rhizomatic book therefore imposes a different order on the flow of ideas, an order without top or bottom, without start or finish. Deleuze and Guattari tell us that 'The rhizome is altogether different, a *map and not a tracing.*'[10] Whereas tracings aspire to be faithful reproductions, maps are open-ended, symbolic representations that require interpretation. More can be read out from a map than was put into it; maps allow for exploration in any and all directions, even beyond their edges, which are, in any case, arbitrary.

The Texte-book

The image of the book as a map resonates with wider post-structuralist thinking. Roland Barthes proposes a series of distinctions not dissimilar to Deleuze and Guattari's root-book and rhizomatic book. Barthes firstly distinguishes between the work and the text:

> The work [*oeuvre*] is a fragment of substance, occupying a part of the space of books (in a library for example), the Text [*Texte*] is a methodological field...the one is displayed, the other demonstrated...the work can be held in the hand, the text is held in language.'[11]

A simplistic reading of this passage might lead to the conclusion that Barthes is using the word 'work' (*oeuvre*) to signify the idea of the physical object that is found in a library, and 'text' (*Texte*) to signify the literary contents of that object. To accept such a simple reduction, however, would be to miss Barthes's point, which is, as I understand it, that *oeuvre* and *Texte* (Barthes capitalizes the word) signify, however nebulously, two different types of book. An oeuvre, Barthes suggests, is not completely synonymous with a book but is a 'fragment of substance' that occupies *part of the space* of the book. An oeuvre is not *itself* a physical object and yet it holds many of the properties of physical objects. An oeuvre is substantive, immutable and enduring; it is 'the object of a consumption',[12] which is to say, it enters into a particular kind of relationship (a contract, perhaps) with its reader where each has certain expectations and obligations. An oeuvre *delivers meaning* in a predictable and consistent way.

A Texte is less tangible than an oeuvre. A Texte appears to us as less of an object and more of a 'methodological field... *experienced only in an activity of production*'.[13] The Texte, unlike the oeuvre, is not consumed, it is produced *in and by the act of reading*; it is a production rather than a product. The Texte is not found *in* a book; it is *what happens* when one reads a certain type of book. Thus 'the Text [*Texte*] cannot stop (for example on a library shelf); its constitutive movement is that of cutting across (in particular, it can cut across the work [*oeuvre*], several works)'.[14] Books may (in a manner of speaking) contain Textes (that is to say, certain conjunctions of books and readers may initiate or release Textes), and yet Textes cannot be contained by books. Every reading of a Texte extends it; that is to say, whenever a Texte is read, a new Texte emerges. Indeed, Barthes went further to suggest that Textes are produced not by their authors (who merely *nourish* their books)[15] but by their readers.

Oeuvres are 'readerly' (*lisible*) insofar as they can be read in only one way; they are amenable to only a single interpretation, the one placed there by the author. The reader, then, 'is left with no more than the poor freedom either to accept or reject [the oeuvre]: reading is nothing more than a referendum'.[16] Textes, on the other hand, are 'writerly' (*scriptible*) to the extent that they are constantly being 'rewritten' each time they are read. Thus 'The Texte is plural. Which is not simply to say that it has several meanings, but that it accomplishes the very plural of meaning: an irreducible plural.'[17] It would be incorrect to think of a Texte as having a specific number of defined or even definable meanings, since it is rewritten each time it is read. A Texte cannot therefore be explicated or summarized, it 'is not a line of words releasing a single "theological" meaning (the "message" of the Author-God) but a multidimensional space in which a variety of writings, none of them original, blend and clash'. Barthes continues: 'The texte is a tissue of quotations drawn from the innumerable centres of culture.'[18]

In order to throw some light on what Barthes might be implying here, we need to remember that the words 'text' (*texte*) and 'tissue' (*tissu*) both originate in the Latin *texere* – to weave. A tissue is a fine gauzy sheer fabric, but also a web or network (as in the expression 'a tissue of lies'). A text is also a woven fabric (a textile), constructed, according to Barthes, from 'quotations without inverted commas'.[19] All writing is, one way or another, an act of weaving together, of reproducing and reiterating what has already been written, with or without inverted commas. Furthermore:

the reader is the space on which all the quotations that make up a writing are inscribed without any of them being lost; a text's unity lies not
in its origin but in its destination.[20]

The book is written by its reader, who is also the space on which the writing
is inscribed. The book, in a (very real) sense, *is* its reader. To build a library
for the paraversity is therefore to build a community of readers (which is to
say, of writers).

Second attempt: in praise of imaginary books

'I repeat: it is enough that a book be possible for it to exist. Only the
impossible is excluded. For example: no book is also a stairway, though
doubtless there are books that discuss and deny and demonstrate this
possibility and others whose structures correspond to that of a stairway.'
Jorge Luis Borges, *The Library of Babel*, 1941

Argentinean poet, essayist and short-story writer Jorge Luis Borges returned
constantly in his work to a number of motifs and images, most notably the
labyrinth, the mirror and the book. Of these, the book was the most potent
and striking (Borges was, after all, for many years the director of the National
Library of Argentina). One of his translators notes that 'Jorge Luis Borges
never wrote anything long and so it is often assumed that he never wrote
much.'[21] It would be tempting also to assume that he never wrote anything
of much worth; that nothing much could be said in the space of a short story
or a 500-word essay. In fact, a deliberate brevity underpinned all of his work,
spanning 60 years and well over 1,000 publications. In the prologue to his
first collection of short stories, in 1941, Borges noted:

The composition of vast books is a laborious and impoverishing extrav-
agance. To go on for five hundred pages developing an idea whose
perfect oral exposition is possible in a few minutes! A better course of
procedure is *to pretend that these books already exist*, and then to offer a
résumé, a commentary.[22]

Many of his short stories and a number of his essays can thus be read as brief
synopses of books that he could not be bothered to write.

Imagined books and imaginary authors

In an early essay, Borges writes in praise of 'verbal labyrinths',[23] of stories
within stories, paintings within paintings, dreams within dreams, and books
within books. Several of his early short stories develop this theme a stage
further by not only mentioning other, often imaginary books by imaginary

authors, but by offering commentaries on them. In his story *An Examination of the Work of Herbert Quain*, Borges reviews the work of an invented novelist, mixing fact and fiction, the real with the imagined.[24] Thus he laments that the eponymous Quain, a fictitious author of fictitious books, is given scarcely half a column for his obituary in the *Times Literary Supplement* (a very real journal), and that *The Spectator* compared Quain's work to that of Agatha Christie and Gertrude Stein. At the end of this short story in the form of a literary essay, Borges confesses that one of Quain's fictitious stories had been the inspiration for Borges's very real story *The Circular Ruins* (which is itself a 'verbal labyrinth' in the form of a dream within a dream).

Borges was also fond of attributing his own literary and philosophical speculations to these imaginary authors. Towards the end of *An Examination of the Works of Herbert Quain*, he suggests that 'Quain was in the habit of arguing that readers were already an extinct species. "Every European," he reasoned, "is a writer, potentially or in fact."' This remarkable statement, written in 1941 and attributed to an imagined writer, prefigured by more than a quarter of a century Roland Barthes's celebrated announcement of 'the death of the author' as the creative force in literature, to be replaced by 'the birth of the reader',[25] that is, by the reader who writes her own meaning into the text as she reads it. However, embedded in a fictional account of a fictitious novelist, Borges's own announcement went unnoticed and unremarked.

Borges employs the same literary device elsewhere. Another story, *The Approach to Al-Mu'tasim*, discusses a novel by 'the Bombay lawyer Mir Bahadur Ali', once again mixing in references to real and imagined critics and publications. As in the case of Herbert Quain, Mir Bahadur and his novel exist only in the mind of Borges, as does Pierre Menard, whose entire published output of monographs, poems and other papers is enumerated and discussed in some depth in Borges's story *Pierre Menard, Author of Don Quixote*. In a similar move, an essay entitled *John Wilkins' Analytical Language* discusses a 'real' historical figure (albeit one whose published output reads like a list from one of Borges's short stories), but with surreptitious references to fictitious books, including a quotation from 'a certain Chinese encyclopedia called the *Heavenly Emporium of Benevolent Knowledge*'.[26]

In each case, Borges's meticulously fabricated back stories to the lives and works of fictitious authors are intended to demonstrate the fluid interplay between the 'textual' world(s) of books and the 'real' world outside of books, anticipating, perhaps, Derrida's (in)famous observation that 'il n'y a pas de hors-texte'.[27] Derrida's point is that there is no external supra-textual vantage point, no way of stepping outside of the web of acknowledged and unacknowledged citations and quotations that comprise *all* texts. Echoing Roland Barthes (somewhat ironically given the context), he adds:

When a text quotes and requotes, with or without quotation marks, when it is written on the brink, you start, or indeed have already started, to lose your footing. You lose sight of any line of demarcation between a text and what is outside it.[28]

The loss of footing engendered by Borges's stories and essays can be seen from the ways in which his fictitious authors and their equally fictitious books and characters have insinuated their way into other books and, occasionally, into the 'real' world *hors-texte*. To give but a few examples: Herbert Quain's fictitious book *The God of the Labyrinth* is discussed by the eponymous and equally fictitious hero in 'real' author José Saramago's novel *The Year of the Death of Ricardo Reis*; The equally real (indeed, larger than life) writer Michel Foucault quotes the passage cited by Borges from the *Heavenly Emporium of Benevolent Knowledge* in the preface to his own book *The Order of Things*, and it is not entirely clear from the context whether or not he considers it to be a *bone fide* reference from a *bone fide* book. And when the story *The Approach to al-Mu'tasim* was first published in 1935, Borges reports that several people who read it took it to be a review of a real book and attempted to order a copy. We can see echoes here of Derrida's much later descent into the abyss of deconstruction, where a 'chain of supplements'[29] leads to what his translator Gayatri Spivak describes as 'an interminable fall' as each reading of a text produces another reading, and so on, and so on, *ad infinitum*. Thus, 'The fall into the abyss of deconstruction inspires us with as much pleasure as fear. We are intoxicated with the prospect of never hitting bottom'.[30]

Curiously, several of Borges's fictitious books have made a full transition *hors-texte* and into the real world. I have suggested already that Foucault was unsure of the provenance of the *Celestial Emporium of Benevolent Knowledge*, and even a cursory search of the internet will reveal a number of websites and blogs that have taken Borges's fiction for reality. For example, in a blog with the rather apt title of *Meandering Wildly*, 'Johnath' reports that 'The book, *Celestial Emporium of Benevolent Knowledge*, is an extremely old Chinese encyclopedia, or so the legend goes, and was translated by a guy named Franz Kuhn.'[31] He adds further that 'A Google search reveals that this book isn't nearly as well known as I would have thought (only 16,000 hits)' and that

I guess it was in one of my philosophy classes – ontology maybe, or philosophy of mind – that I first heard about it, but in a 4 year cog sci degree you can't avoid hearing about this book half a dozen times. It comes up virtually any time you get into a conversation about classifications, taxonomies or crazy people.

More curious still, Borges had already anticipated this seeping of fiction into the world of facts. In a story from 1940 entitled *Tlön, Uqbar, Orbis Tertius*, he imagines a secret society of writers, scientists and philosophers who wrote and published a complete 40-volume set of encyclopaedias detailing every aspect of an imaginary world named Tlön. The encyclopaedias included:

> the complete history of an unknown planet, with its architecture and its playing cards, its mythological terrors and the sound of its dialects, its emperors and its oceans, its minerals, its birds, and its fishes, its algebra and its fire, its theological and metaphysical arguments, all clearly stated, coherent, without any apparent dogmatic intention or parodic undertone.

Borges's story relates how certain aspects of the 'real world' began to take on the properties of the fictional world of Tlön, sometimes in striking and seemingly impossible ways. The story ends with a lengthy 'postscript', dated 1947, but published as part of the original story in 1941. This postscript recounted how, in the years following the discovery of the encyclopaedias and other 'Tlönian' artefacts, and even after the revelation that they had been 'planted' as part of a deliberate hoax:

> the international Press overwhelmingly hailed the 'find'. Manuals, anthologies, summaries, literal versions, authorized reprints, and pirated editions of the Master Work of Man poured and continue to pour out into the world. Almost immediately, reality gave ground on more than one point. The truth is that it hankered to give ground.

In Borges's story, a series of books detailing an imagined and imaginary world, and one which its readers knew to be imagined, imposed itself so violently on the real one that, before long, it had almost completely overturned objective and material reality. Thus, Borges concludes:

> Now, the conjectural 'primitive language' of Tlön has found its way into the schools. Now, the teaching of its harmonious history, full of stirring episodes, has obliterated the history which dominated my childhood. Now, in all memories, a fictitious past occupies the place of any other. We know nothing about it with any certainty, not even that it is false. Numismatics, pharmacology, and archaeology have been revised. I gather that biology and mathematics are awaiting their avatar... Then, English, French, and mere Spanish will disappear from this planet. The world will be Tlön.

It would be difficult to conceive a more powerful and persuasive argument for the transformative potential of the book. Furthermore, the fact that this account is itself published in a book is hardly coincidental; it would be hard to imagine a film, a piece of music, a poem or a play being able to supplant reality in even a modest way.[32]

The total library

Perhaps the strangest of all of Borges's imaginary books appears much later in his writing career. In 1975, he published a short 1,500-word story entitled *The Book of Sand*, which in typical Borgesian fashion, begins with the words:

> The line is made up of an infinite number of points; the plane of an infinite number of lines; the volume of an infinite number of planes . . . No, unquestionably this is not – *more geometrico* – the best way of beginning my story. To claim that it is true is nowadays the convention of every made-up story. Mine, however, *is* true.[33]

This is, of course, *precisely* the best way to begin his story; a reference to abstract geometry and calculus and a postmodern claim (by the time of writing this story, postmodern literary theory had just about caught up with Borges) that, unlike most 'made-up stories', this one is true. The story goes on to describe a late-night visit from 'a tall man with nondescript features' who offers to sell the narrator (who, perhaps, is Borges himself) 'a holy book that I came across on the outskirts of Bikaner'.[34] As the narrator inspects it, he realizes that it is no ordinary book:

> I opened the book at random. The script was strange to me. The pages, which were worn and typographically poor, were laid out in double columns, as in a Bible. The text was closely printed, and it was ordered in versicles. In the upper corners of the pages were Arabic numbers. I noticed that one left-hand page bore the number (let us say) 40,514 and the facing right-hand page 999. I turned the leaf; it was numbered with eight digits. It also bore a small illustration, like the kind used in dictionaries – an anchor drawn with pen and ink, as if by a schoolboy's clumsy hand. It was at this point that the stranger said, 'Look at the illustration closely. You'll never see it again.'[35]

As the story progresses, it emerges that 'the number of pages in this book is no more or less than infinite'.[36]

The Book of Sand is, in fact, a distillation and a simplification of one of Borges's much earlier stories called *The Library of Babel*, which itself developed from a short three-page essay, written in 1939, entitled *The Total Library*. This essay traces the philosophical origins (using, as far as I am aware, 'real' sources) of the idea that the random arrangement of the letters of the alphabet would, sooner or later, reproduce every book that has ever been written and, far more significantly, every book that *could possibly* be written.[37] Borges adds that 'The totality of such variations would form a Total Library of astronomical size.'[38]

The story *The Library of Babel*, written two years after this essay, begins thus:

The universe (which others call the Library) is composed of an indefinite, perhaps an infinite, number of hexagonal galleries, with enormous ventilation shafts in the middle, encircled by very low railings.

He continues:

Five shelves correspond to each one of the walls of each hexagon; each shelf contains thirty-two books of a uniform format; each book is made up of four hundred and ten pages; each page, of forty lines; each line, of some eighty black letters.

Most of the books in the library comprise a random jumble of letters, but occasionally a book would be found that contained one or more comprehensible words. The narrator tells of a book which his father saw which 'was composed of the letters MCV perversely repeated from the first line to the last'. Another is 'a mere labyrinth of letters' apart from the sentence on the next-to-last page, 'O time your pyramids'. Over the years, the inhabitants of the Library came to understand that 'all the books, however diverse, are made up of uniform elements: the period, the comma, the space, the 22 letters of the alphabet'. From these 'incontrovertible premises' it was deduced:

that the Library is total and that its shelves contain all the possible combinations of the twenty-odd orthographical symbols (whose number, though vast, is not infinite); that is, everything which can be expressed, in all languages. Everything is there: the minute history of the future, the autobiographies of the archangels, the faithful catalogue of the Library, thousands and thousands of false catalogues, a demonstration of the fallacy of these catalogues, a demonstration of the fallacy of the true catalogue, the Gnostic gospel of Basilides, the commentary on this gospel, the veridical account of your death, a version of each book in all languages, the interpolations of every book in all books.

It is perhaps worth re-reading the above passage and pausing to consider its implications. Whilst the story is, of course, a work of fiction, the *idea* (and thus the possibility) of the Total Library is very real.

Borges reports that when it was realized that the Library contained every possible book, 'the first impression was of extravagant joy'. In what appears to be an analogy to the Enlightenment project, he continues: 'All men felt themselves lords of a secret, intact treasure. There was no personal or universal problem whose eloquent solution did not exist – in some hexagon.' Thus:

The clarification of the basic mysteries of humanity – the origin of the Library and of time – was also expected. It is credible that those grave mysteries can be explained in words: if the language of the philosophers does not suffice, the multiform Library will have produced the unexpected language required and the necessary vocabularies and grammars for this language.

However, disillusionment quickly set in. How could it ever be possible to distinguish the 'true' history of the future from the millions of 'false' ones; the faithful catalogue of the library from all of the false catalogues; the demonstration of the fallacy of these catalogues from the demonstration of the fallacy of this demonstration? As is often the case in Borges's stories, there is no solution other than despair and resignation: 'the certainty that everything has been already written nullifies or makes phantoms of us all'.

The last and final word

In this final chapter, I have posed the question What is a book? and suggested some possible ways of thinking about an answer. That particular question inevitably led to others, such as What is a book for?, How might we read a book?, What can a book tell us? and What are the limits of a book? There are, as far as I can tell, no specific or definitive answers to any of these questions, but some of the thoughts encountered along the way included the idea of a book as a 'little machine', as a kind of map, as a nebulous gauzy textile and as a dispenser of infinite but unverifiable knowledge. Deleuze and Guattari helped us to understand the rhizomatic structure of the book, which mirrors the structure of the paraversity; Barthes intimated that the book and its readers are one and the same, which is to say, perhaps, that the construction of the paraversity is the construction of a community of readers; and Borges alerted us to the dangers of 'the febrile library, whose hazardous volumes run the constant risk of being changed into others and in which everything is affirmed, denied, and confused as by a divinity in delirium',[39] surely a huge problem for library cataloguers.

The starting point for this particular book was Bill Readings' thesis of 'The University in Ruins', and it is therefore apt and fitting that he should have the last (but not the final) word. In his book *Introducing Lyotard*, Readings presents the *act of reading* as an *incitement to act*, that is, as both a practical and a moral undertaking. The purpose of reading a book is not merely to understand the meaning of a text, nor simply and passively to agree or disagree with it: 'Reading is not a matter of mimetic representation or conceptual critique: it is an ethical practice . . . Reading should *do justice* to a text.'[40] And for Readings, doing justice does not entail asking what a text means or signifies; the question is rather 'What demand does the text make? How am I addressed by it?';[41] and, of course, doing justice also means *responding* to that demand. Clearly, then, the conclusion of this particular book is not an end, not a last word, but a starting place for the real work of building the paraversity as a community of dissensus 'where thought takes place beside thought, where thinking is a shared process without identity or unity'.[42] And so, at last, to Jacques Derrida for the final (but not the last) word: 'For there *must* not be a last word – that's what I'd like to say finally.'[43]

Notes

Preface

1. Readings capitalizes the word 'University' where he is referring to the institution as a whole rather than to individual universities. He continues this convention when he makes reference to, for example, the University of Excellence and the post-historical university. He also capitalizes certain other terms such as Thought and Cultural Studies in cases where he intends them to be regarded as proper nouns.
2. Readings 1996, p.10.
3. Ibid., p.22, his emphasis.
4. Ibid., p.11.
5. Ibid., p.24.
6. Ibid.
7. Ibid., p.133.
8. Ibid., p.12.
9. Natasha Lehrer, *Jerusalem Post*, cited in Readings, op. cit.
10. Readings, op. cit., pp.192–3.

I The academy in peril

1. Many of these changes can be traced in the UK to the *Charter for Higher Education 1993*, which explicitly employed the language and terminology of the marketplace. For example: 'Universities and colleges are more and more aware of the need to *deliver* high-quality *services*, responding to the *needs* and *demands* of *customers.'* Department for Education 1993, my emphasis.
2. Furedi 2004, p.12. Although Furedi's book begins from much the same point as mine, our arguments develop in very different directions. Indeed, Furedi would probably regard me and many of the writers I cite as part of the problem of the 'dumbing down' of society rather than part of the solution.
3. Readings 1996, p.2.
4. For a more comprehensive account, see Graham 2008 for what he calls 'a very short history of universities in Britain and abroad'.
5. Readings, op. cit., p.14. He warns, however, that 'the historical narrative that I propose (reason-culture-excellence) is not simply a sequential one'.
6. Humboldt 1970.
7. Readings, op. cit., p.5.
8. Ibid., p.64.
9. Ibid., p.12.
10. Lyotard 1979. Lyotard's thesis is that knowledge is organized and disseminated

through narratives or language games of various types. Traditionally, these 'little narratives' communicate knowledge in keeping with a particular set of rules and shared conventions about what can be said, in what form, and the relationship between the speaker and the listener. Lyotard points out that, in most little narratives, it is the receiver of the message who bestows validity or legitimation upon it. However, he also identifies a number of 'grand narratives' that claim a universal status, which attempts to account for and subsume all little narratives. One of the features of a grand narrative is that the validity or legitimation of the message is contained within the narrative itself and does not rely on the accept-ance and assent of the listener. In other words, a grand narrative not only relates a story about knowledge, but also a 'metadiscourse' about why the knowledge is true. The grand narratives of truth and emancipation are those 'self-evident' stories told by modern western society to underpin and legitimate the (usually scientific) quest for knowledge.

11. Ibid., p.31.
12. Ibid., p.34.
13. John Keats, *Ode on a Grecian Urn*.
14. This quotation is much attributed but, to the best of my knowledge, never refer-enced.
15. This might, on first glance, appear to be a rather odd definition of the term 'fact', which is nowadays usually associated with truth rather than being placed in opposition to it. However, the dictionary defines a fact merely as 'an actual event or occurrence' and 'a piece of information', derived from the Latin *facere*, to make. The term 'fact' therefore relates to surface appearance, or in phenomeno-logical terms, to 'sense data', and it is this meaning that is contrasted with underlying essence, reality or 'truth'.
16. Lyotard, op. cit., p.35.
17. Ibid., p.36.
18. Comte 1830, p.2, my emphasis.
19. It could be argued, however, that whereas the nineteenth-century positivism of Comte took little interest in hidden or final causes, twentieth-century science, particularly particle physics, has taken on the challenge of the grand narrative of truth, and, like the arts, is concerned with the search for essence, with ultimate understanding, with what Stephen Hawking characterized as 'the mind of God'.
20. Snow 1959.
21. Snow points out: 'A good many times I have been present at gatherings of people who, by the standards of the traditional culture, are thought highly educated and who have with considerable gusto been expressing their incredulity at the illiteracy of scientists. Once or twice I have been provoked and have asked the company how many of them could describe the Second Law of Thermodynamics. The response was cold: it was also negative. Yet I was asking something which is the scientific equivalent of: *Have you read a work of Shakespeare's?* I now believe that if I had asked an even simpler question – such as, What do you mean by mass, or acceleration, which is about the scientific equivalent of saying, *Can you read?* – not more than one in ten of the highly educated would have felt that I was speaking the same language. So the great edifice of modern physics goes up, and the majority of the cleverest people in the western world have about as much insight into it as their neolithic ancestors would have had' (ibid., pp.14–15).
22. Readings, op. cit., p.70.
23. Ibid.
24. Lyotard 1983.
25. Readings, op. cit., p.12.

26. Readings pointed to the rise of Cultural Studies as a *bona fide* academic subject as proof of this point. He claimed that cultural studies is only viable as a distinct course of study if the promulgation of culture is no longer the primary and over-arching aim of the university.

27. Readings 1991, p.22. We might, unfortunately, add a number of other examples in the years since Readings made this observation.

28. In 1949, with the horrors of Nazi Germany still fresh in his mind, the German philosopher, musician and critical theorist Theodor Adorno proclaimed that 'to write poetry after Auschwitz is barbaric' (Adorno 1951, p.34). He later added that 'it may have been wrong to say that after Auschwitz you could no longer write poems. But it is not wrong to raise the less cultural question whether after Auschwitz you can go on living...' (Adorno 1966, pp.362–3). Both Lyotard and Readings appear to be developing Adorno's assertion that totalitarianism in general, and Nazism in particular, was the natural and inevitable consequence of the Enlightenment project, which has replaced uncertainty and superstition with 'the disenchantment of the world' through calculative rationality. Thus, although the aims of the Enlightenment were 'always aimed at liberating men from fear and establishing their sovereignty... the fully enlightened earth radi-ates disaster triumphant' (Adorno 1947, p.3).

29. Stefan Collini characterizes the history of the university as follows: 'In the long march that has seen universities function as seminaries, finishing schools, govern-ment staff colleges, depositories of culture, nurseries of citizenship, and centres of scientific research, they were now to turn themselves into plcs' (Collini 2012, p.34).

30. Whilst postmodernism has been defined in numerous different (and sometimes conflicting) ways, I broadly support Lyotard in his statement that 'Simplifying to the extreme, I define *postmodern* as incredulity toward metanarratives' (Lyotard 1979, p.xxiv). This assertion that we should not take the self-validation claims of the Enlightenment grand narratives at face value supports his contentions else-where that postmodernism is not a successor to modernism (it is not, he says, the next modernism) but rather an ongoing critique or repudiation of it.

31. Recent economic events have perhaps called the blind acceptance of market forces into question.

32. Readings 1996, p.6.

33. Ibid., his emphasis.

34. I am tempted here to borrow Readings' phrase when he writes of 'banal and cliché-ridden mission statements (which are all the same from university to university)' (ibid., p.133).

35. Ibid., p.120.

36. Quality Assurance Agency for Higher Education 2000, p.18.

37. More recently, the Performance Based Review Fund (PBRF) in New Zealand, the Research Quality Framework (RQF) in Australia, and similar schemes in Hong Kong and The Netherlands.

38. At the time of writing, the RAE is in the process of being replaced by a new Research Excellence Framework (REF). This promises to base the assessment of research quality even more firmly on quantitative indicators, and (as witnessed by the change in title) clearly and explicitly buys into the 'excellence' agenda.

39. The sociologist C. Wright Mills anticipated the rise of impersonal production-line research more than half a century ago in his appeal to the 'intellectual craftsman' to 'stand for the primacy of the individual scholar; stand opposed to the ascendancy of research teams of technicians. Be one mind that it is on its own confronting the problems of man and society' (Mills 1959, p.246).

40. Drucker 1994.

41. For example, Leisure and Tourism Studies, Sports Studies and Nursing Studies. It could be argued that the word 'studies' in their titles signals the fact that these are not, of themselves, academic subjects. This point will be explored further in Chapter 2.

42. Usher 2002, p.145. Usher's statement would seem to imply that knowledge is no longer merely a commodity to be bought and sold in the knowledge economy, but has now become the unit of currency.

43. Newman 1858, p.xxxvii, his emphasis.

44. Graham, op. cit., p.46. Even the doctorate, now regarded as a research training, takes its name from the Latin *doctoris*, meaning 'teacher' and was traditionally awarded in recognition of a life dedicated to learning and scholarship, and later as a licence to teach.

45. Scott 1984, p.54. Indeed, as early as 1958 the University Grants Committee in the UK detected 'an atmosphere in which it is almost taken for granted that to take place in scientific research is the highest destiny of man'. They continued, somewhat prophetically (and perhaps a little indignantly), that 'We have heard it suggested that the standard of a university institution is measurable by the amount of research which is done there' (University Grants Committee 1958).

46. As we saw above, John Henry Newman considered research to be outside the scope of the early Modern University. When he claimed the purpose of the university to be the pursuit of knowledge, he was referring to the pursuit and acquisition of *existing* knowledge rather than the generation of new knowledge.

47. Readings, op. cit., p.67.

48. Ritzer 2004.

49. The Credit Accumulation and Transfer Scheme (CATS) is a points system recognized by all UK higher education institutions as a method of quantifying credit for a particular module or programme. CATS points can be accumulated towards an academic award or can be 'cashed in' as exemption from certain modules.

50. Bauman 1997, p.23.

51. Ibid., p.23.

52. Boyer 1990. Peter Scott suggests somewhat cynically that 'the PhD was a new-fangled idea reluctantly introduced to wean wealthy Americans off the universities of Germany' (Scott, op. cit., p.3).

53. Modern notions of *science* and *scientists* date only to the nineteenth century (Webster's Ninth New Collegiate Dictionary dates the origin of the word 'scientist' to 1834). Before then, the word 'science' simply meant knowledge.

54. Graham, op. cit., p.92, his emphasis.

55. Previous generations of scientists had generally managed to resist these challenges to 'pure' or 'blue skies' research. When asked in the early nineteenth century about the possible uses of electromagnetism, Michael Faraday is reported to have responded with the question: 'What use is a newborn child?' A more recent and more prosaic example cites 'non-stick frying pans' as the answer to the question 'What was the point of sending a man to the moon?'

56. Forscher 1963.

57. As Roland Barthes pointed out, 'Some people talk avidly, demandingly of method; what they want in a work is method, which can never be too rigorous or too formal for their taste . . . ' (Barthes 1971a, pp.200–1).

58. Sorell 1991, p.1.

59. Adorno 1962, p.19.

60. Habermas 1968, p.4.

61. Tallis 2000.

62. Ibid., p.324.

63. Ibid., p.321.

64. Ibid., p.326.
65. Heidegger 1938, p.125, my emphasis.
66. Boyer, op. cit., p.15.
67. Ibid.
68. Ibid.
69. HEFC 2006.
70. My own university is one such institution. Its definition of scholarship is even more extreme than that offered by the HEFC, and includes:
   • Reading relevant literature
   • Training courses
   • Maintaining professional or clinical skills
   • Time spent at other institutions to keep up-to-date in field of expertise and/or sharing best practice
   • Attending general professional development conferences (but not those relating to specific research areas or projects)
   • Private consultancy carried out in University time and done with its agreement, if it contributes to the maintenance and development of clinical or professional skills.
71. Andreson 2000.
72. Barnett 2005, p.4.
73. Elam 1966, Foreword to *The University in Ruins*.
74. Readings 1996, p.20.
75. Ibid., p. 179. As we shall see in the next chapter, the capitalization of the word 'Thought' is deliberate.

2 Thinking as a subversive activity

1. Readings 1996, p.46.
2. I will revisit this argument later when I discuss the rise of cultural studies.
3. Ibid., p.169. Readings' decision to use the word 'dwell' possibly derives from Heidegger, and will be examined in greater detail in Chapter 3.
4. Ibid., p.170.
5. Ibid., p.170–1.
6. Ibid., p.122. As we know, the word 'university' derives neither from an association with unity nor universality, but from the Latin *universitas*, a medieval legal association or guild. Readings' notion of the 'University with no idea' can be seen, at least in part, as a response to a number of books and papers on the theme of the 'idea of a university', including works by John Henry Newman, Michael Oakeshott, Jürgen Habermas, Karl Jaspers and Peter Scott. In fact, Habermas traces the term back to Humboldt.
7. Ibid.
8. Ibid., p.160.
9. Ibid., p.159.
10. Ibid., p.160.
11. Ibid., his emphasis. A similar point is made by Alain Badiou: 'A genuine philosopher is someone who decides on his own accord what the important problems are, someone who proposes new problems for everyone' (Badiou 2005, p.2).
12. Ibid.
13. Barthes 1966b. Barthes was referring to writing rather than thought.
14. I realize that I appear to be treating 'thoughts' as more or less tangible objects, albeit objects that are regarded by the University of Excellence as so much waste. This, of course, is a natural consequence of regarding the mission of the university in terms of product rather than process.

15. Readings, op. cit., p.18, his emphasis.
16. Foucault 1981, p.155.
17. Readings, op. cit., p.175.
18. Ibid.
19. Alain Badiou, in his *Second Manifesto for Philosophy*, looks forward to the 'return of the affirmative power of the idea' in order to challenge the view 'that thinking serves no purpose and even proves harmful' (Badiou 2009, pp. 5–6).
20. Kant 1798.
21. Readings, op. cit., p.16.
22. See, for example, Foucault 1978.
23. Kant makes the distinction between 'scholastic' philosophy, that is philosophy as a discipline similar to other academic disciplines, and philosophy as a *conceptus cosmicus*, 'the science of the relation of all knowledge to the essential ends of human reason' (Kant 1787, p.657).
24. Readings, op. cit., p.57, my emphasis.
25. The educationalist Peter Scott suggests that history briefly took over as the 'key discipline' in the liberal university at the end of the nineteenth century, only to be replaced by English literature after the First World War (Scott 1984, pp.31–32).
26. Scott suggests that philosophy also alienated itself from mainstream academic thought, to the extent that 'the abstractions of philosophy could never have appealed to the broader intellectual constituency that the universities had begun to serve by the beginning of the twentieth century' (ibid., pp.31–32).
27. Readings, op. cit., p.70.
28. Schlegel 1841, p.9.
29. Newman 1858, p.113.
30. Ibid., p.193.
31. Snow 1959, p.4.
32. Leavis 1969, pp.59–60.
33. Readings, op. cit., p.16.
34. Habermas 1968, p.4. As Theodor Adorno puts it: 'The most patent expression of philosophy's historical fate is the way the special sciences compelled it to turn back into a special science' (Adorno 1966, p.4).
35. Wittgenstein 1922, 4.121, his emphasis.
36. Ibid., 4.3.
37. Ibid., 6.54.
38. Ibid., 7.
39. Ibid., 4.111.
40. Wittgenstein 1953, p.114.
41. See pp.11–12 for Wittgenstein's list of language games.
42. Slavoj Žižek rather pithily puts it thus: 'Name me a single example of a successful philosophical dialogue that wasn't a dreadful misunderstanding...Aristotle didn't understand Plato correctly; Hegel – who might have been pleased by the fact – of course didn't understand Kant. And Heidegger fundamentally didn't understand anyone at all' (Žižek 2005, p.50).
43. Saussure 1916.
44. Wittgenstein 1953, p.220.
45. Readings gives a more anglocentric account of the rise of literature that takes in F.R. Leavis and the so-called New Critics. However, it seems to me that the largely Francophone project of post-structuralist literary criticism has had a far greater impact on the wider academy not only in France but also in the English-speaking world.
46. Barthes 1963.
47. Barthes 1964a.

48. Indeed, this outward expansion of the discipline of literature and literary studies is later made explicit. In his inaugural lecture to the *Collège de France* in 1977, Barthes stated that, 'I mean by literature neither a body nor a series of works, nor even a branch of commerce or a teaching, but the complex graph of the traces of a practice, *the practice of writing*' (Barthes 1977, p.462, my emphasis). This might be seen as an audacious attempt to position literary criticism as a general critique of all writing, by which I mean the *practice* of writing as an academic endeavour. Clearly, such a move would have radical and extreme implications for the ways that the academy makes judgements, for example, on publications submitted to the UK Research Excellence Framework (see Chapter 1).
49. Picard 1965. This title is echoed in the later critique of post-structuralism by Alan Sokal and Jean Bricmont entitled *Impostures Intellectuelles*.
50. Barthes 1966a.
51. Ibid., p.3, his emphasis. Of course, Wittgenstein would no doubt point out that to talk of language is also to use it.
52. Ibid., p.3.
53. Ibid.
54. Ibid.
55. Ibid., p.4, his emphasis.
56. Ibid.
57. Fernandez-Armesto 1997, p.177.
58. Scruton 2004.
59. Thus: 'In the Anglo-Saxon world especially, logical positivism, first inaugurated in the Viennese school, has gained ground to the point of virtual monopoly. In the sense that it is modern by reason of its remarkably consistent faculty of enlightenment, it strikes many as the doctrine most suited to the needs of a technological and scientifically-minded era' (Adorno 1962, p.12).
60. Verificationism is one of the central principles of logical positivism that associates the meaning of a proposition with its method of verification. Verificationism immediately rules out all metaphysical propositions and becomes even more restrictive in the hands of certain positivists and analytical philosophers who conflate epistemology with the scientific method.
61. Smith *et al.* 1992.
62. Smith 1994, p.i.
63. See, for example, Sokal and Bricmont 1998.
64. Readings, op. cit., p.91.
65. Ibid., p.91.
66. Ibid.
67. Ibid., p.17.
68. Ibid.
69. Ibid.
70. Ibid.
71. Eagleton 1996, p.12.
72. Readings, op. cit., p.171.
73. Ibid.
74. I could, I suppose, have used the term 'subversity' rather than paraversity to denote its underground and subversive nature. In a similar vein, Clark Kerr had much earlier coined the term 'multiversity' to describe the ever-growing span and reach of activities that the title 'university', to some extent, belies. But whereas the contrast between the university and the multiversity is that of the singular and the many, the contrast I hope to highlight between the university and the paraversity is between convergent and parallel thinking; consensus and dissensus (Kerr 1963).

75. See Lyotard 1987, pp.8–9: 'Postmodernity is not a new age, it is the rewriting of some features modernity had tried or pretended to gain . . .'.
76. Readings op. cit., p.46.
77. Ibid., p.192.

Part 2 Building the paraversity

1. Barnett 2000, p.2, his emphasis.
2. Readings, 1996, p.2.

3 The philosophy of dissensus

1. Readings 1996, p.169.
2. Ibid., p.172.
3. Brewer 2008, p.179.
4. Ibid., p.182.
5. Ibid., p.195.
6. Ibid., p.229.
7. Ibid., p.184.
8. Heidegger 1951, pp.347–63.
9. Ibid., p.347.
10. Ibid., p.350. This etymological approach is typical of Heidegger's later work. Through a series of speculative leaps, Heidegger manages to associate *wohnen* (to dwell) with *sein* (to be), thereby allowing him to reach the conclusion that 'Dwelling is the manner in which mortals are on the Earth' (p.350). Jacques Derrida performs a similar operation on the French verb *demeure* but makes the etymological leap in the opposite direction towards *meurt* (death) (Derrida 1992a, pp.77–79).
11. Heidegger, op. cit., p.350, his emphasis.
12. Ibid., p.361, his emphasis.
13. Heidegger 1955, p.46.
14. Ibid., p.45, his emphasis.
15. Ibid., p.56, his emphasis.
16. Ibid., p.46.
17. Readings, op. cit., p.160.
18. Heidegger 1955, p.53.
19. We should be careful, however, not to pursue the similarities between meditative thinking and the name of Thought too far. Heidegger's project was metaphysical in intent, whereas Readings wished explicitly to avoid what he called 'a metaphysical transcendence' (Readings, op. cit., p.159).
20. Readings, op. cit., p.2.
21. Heidegger 1951, p.349.
22. Readings, op. cit., p.192.
23. Ibid., p.122.
24. Readings implies, however, that the term 'community of dissensus' could be seen as an oxymoron, since the modern(ist) idea of community is based precisely upon open and transparent communication, and communication in turn requires that 'the singularity or difference of others is reduced' (ibid., p.182).
25. Ibid., p.127.
26. In any case, as Derrida points out, we do not yet know how the words 'yes' and 'no' operate in language, and neither should we assume that they take on opposite meanings. Derrida 1987.
27. Readings, op. cit., p.188. The French philosopher and cultural critic Jacques

Rancière also employed the term 'dissensus', albeit with a somewhat different meaning. As well as drawing attention to the difference between consensus and dissensus, Rancière also played on the literal meaning of the term as a 'disruption of the sensible' or an 'interruption of the ways in which we establish the criteria of knowledge' (see Panagia 2010, p.98). For Panagia, this is a deeply political move, such that 'Rancière wants to wrest democratic political action from the demand that it correspond to a form of authoritative knowledge that will legitimate it' (ibid., p.98).

28. Despite Lyotard's observation that 'the pronoun of the first-person plural is, in effect, the lynchpin of/for the discourse of authorization', it is, of course, impossible to avoid using it (Lyotard 1983, p.98). However, when I use the word 'we' in this book, I would wish it to be understood in the *collective* sense of referring to a plurality of singular *persons* united by a particular social bond rather than to the notion of a singular *people* (see Readings, op. cit., p.190).

29. The term 'singularities' is borrowed from Jean-Luc Nancy, who explores ways of speaking in and of the plurality of the 'we' whilst avoiding making the 'we' a singular identity (Nancy 1996).

30. Readings, op. cit., p.190.

31. Deleuze and Guattari 1980, p.15.

32. Ibid., p.21.

33. Ibid., pp.6–7.

34. Readings, op. cit., p.177.

35. Ibid., p.191. Readings' 'shifting disciplinary structure' shares a number of similarities with Gibbons' distinction between Mode 1 and Mode 2 knowledge production. Mode 2 knowledge production assumes a transdisciplinarity that challenges the very idea of disciplines, and which 'is essentially a temporary configuration and thus highly mutable. It takes its particular shape and generates the content of its theoretical and methodological core in response to problem-formulations that occur in highly specific and local contexts of application' (Gibbons *et al.* 1994, pp.29–30).

36. Deleuze and Guattari, op. cit., p.25.

37. Ibid.

38. Ibid.

39. Ibid., p.12, their emphasis.

40. Readings, op. cit., p.66.

41. Kant 1798, pp.27–9. It is important to note that when Kant associates science (*Wissenschaftlichen*) with truth (*Wahrheit*), both words lose many of their nuances when translated into English. The German noun *Wissenschaft* refers broadly to the systematic pursuit of knowledge rather than specifically to the method of science, whilst *Wahrheit* has links not only to the English word 'truth' but also to 'verification', that is to empirical evidence or proof. In fact, Habermas suggests that 'The word "Wissenschaft" has accumulated such rich connotations that there is no simple equivalent for it in English or French' (Habermas 1986, p.109).

42. Kant's faculty of philosophy contained two departments: 'a department of *historical knowledge* (including history, geography, philology and the humanities, along with all the empirical knowledge contained in the natural sciences), and a department of *pure rational knowledge* (pure mathematics and pure philosophy, the metaphysics of nature and of morals)' (Kant 1798, p.45, his emphasis). It is the latter department to which Kant devotes most of his attention, and with which we are concerned here.

43. Kant 1787, p.657.

44. Kant 1798, p.43.

45. Readings, op.cit., p.57.
46. Ibid., p.173. Alain Badiou refers rather disparagingly to this newly revived interest in ethics as a 'social substitute' for philosophy and as 'the most elementary form of moralizing preaching' (Badiou 2009, p.68).
47. Kant 1787, p.658, my emphasis. It is important to note that, for Kant, philosophy stands apart from most other 'faculties' in the university. Philosophy has no content, it is not a subject to be studied, but is a system or a way of thinking. Thus: 'we cannot learn philosophy ... We can only learn to philosophize, that is, to exercise the talent of reason' (ibid., p.657).
48. Lyotard 1983, p.xiii.
49. Ibid.
50. Ibid., p.xiv.
51. Ibid., p.xii.
52. Ibid., p.xi.
53. Readings 1991.
54. Ibid., p.118.
55. Ibid.
56. Ibid., p.123.
57. Lyotard, op. cit., p.142.
58. Ibid., p.149.
59. Ibid., p.158.
60. Readings 1996, p.192.

4 Being subversive

1. Readings 1996, p.159. He adds: 'In the University of Excellence, the problem of value is bracketed, and statistical evaluation (of the measure of excellence) is presumed to provide definitive answers that then feed into funding, resources, and salary decisions' (ibid., pp.150–1).
2. Derrida 1996, p.218. Lyotard proposed a similar approach to deconstruction with his concept of paralogy, which stands in opposition to the scientific practice of the legitimation of knowledge by and through the dominant paradigm and suggests in its place 'a model of legitimation that has nothing to do with maximized performance, but has as its basis difference understood as paralogy' (Lyotard 1979, p.60). Paralogy, like deconstruction, is subversive, unsettling and divisive. It calls into question the practice of consensus by demonstrating the impossibility of a single, finite 'end' to knowledge.
3. Derrida 1967a, p.158.
4. Mill 1833, pp.56–7.
5. Collini 2012, p.133.
6. Readings, op.cit., p.133.
7. Ibid., p.12. The extent to which the institution of the university has signed up to the values of the corporate business world is reflected by the decision of the Higher Education Funding Council of England (HEFCE) to fund a £250,000 research project to encourage universities to promote institutional 'distinctiveness'. Tricia Scott, research leader for the project, suggested that universities conduct 'brand audits' and develop new 'mottoes' and mission statements in order 'to stand out in an age of greater competition', pointing to Ikea and Brains brewery as examples of successful branding (reported in *Times Higher Education*, 8 September 2011, p.11). The political philosopher Michael Oakeshott would most certainly have taken issue with this view, having pointed out 60 years previously that 'it would be necessary for a university to advertise itself as pursuing a particular purpose only if it were talking to people so ignorant

that they had to be spoken to in baby language, or if it were so little confident of its power to embrace those who came to it that it had to call attention to incidental charms' (Oakeshott 1950, p.106).

8. Melody 1997, p.82.

9. Whilst I am aware that the device of taking examples from one's own institution to illustrate general points is hardly new, I was nonetheless surprised to come across a previously published book more or less devoted to a critique of my own university. Written following what the authors refer to in inverted commas as their 'voluntary redundancy', Duke Maskell and Ian Robinson's book *The New Idea of a University* is a glorious rant (in the best possible sense) and a withering condemnation of the demise of liberal education in the UK, lavishly illustrated with examples taken from their time working as academics in the English department at University College Swansea, now Swansea University. Whilst they acknowledge that, 'We write straight out of first-hand experience of a very few institutions and of one subject', they defend this anecdotal approach with the observation that English Literature 'itself consists of anecdotes raised to the level of art' (Maskell and Robinson 2001, pp. vii–viii).

10. Swansea University *Strategic Plan 2009–14.*

11. It is instructive to compare this 'educational' mission with that of the same institution from 1993, which stated that 'The Objects of the College shall be to provide...all branches of a liberal education' (University College of Swansea Charter and Statutes, cited in Maskell and Robinson, op. cit., p.ii). A decade later, Charles Clarke, the Education Secretary for the UK government, told an academic audience: 'I don't mind there being some mediaevalists for ornamental purposes, but there is no reason for the state to pay for them' (reported in *The Guardian*, Saturday 10 May 2003, p.3). Unsurprisingly, a Professor of Mediaeval History at Kings College reportedly described these comments as 'crudely utilitarian and materialist'. Of course, it was not only mediaevalists who fell into Clarke's category of 'ornaments', and almost every university in the country has since experienced the closure of one or more departments lacking in what Clarke referred to as 'clear usefulness'. As Maskell and Robinson had observed only two years previously, liberal education, education for its own sake, was unlikely to survive into the twenty-first century. They added somewhat poignantly, 'We think this matters' (Maskell and Robinson, op. cit., p. vii).

12. Swansea University *Strategic Plan 2009–14.* However, the most recent *Times Higher Education World University Rankings* tells a different story, with my university being awarded a score of 17.6 per cent for teaching and 18.1 per cent for research.

13. In fact, it would appear to relate to the finding from the NSS that 85 per cent of students responded positively to the statement 'staff are enthusiastic about what they are teaching'. It is perhaps somewhat disingenuous to extrapolate from this score any numerical value relating to 'the enthusiasm of staff'. Certainly, no academic or student with any training or experience in social research would derive such a claim from these data.

14. Ibid.

15. Newman 1858, pp.109–10.

16. Robbins 1963, p.6.

17. Ibid., p.7.

18. National Committee of Inquiry into Higher Education 1997.

19. Department for Education and Skills 2003, p.39.

20. Roper 2005, p.4.

21. Department of Trade and Industry 2000, p.27.

22. Swansea University *Strategic Plan 2009–14.* The development of a new 'Science

and Innovation Campus' in my university might perhaps be seen as a particular example of the second stage of a general move in the UK (and probably elsewhere) to separate the teaching mission from the mission of the generation and financial exploitation of knowledge. The first stage of this move has been (at least in some faculties and departments) the functional and structural separation of teaching from research and teachers from researchers. The second stage, as we have seen, is the move towards a physical separation of teaching and 'knowledge exploitation' onto different campuses; and the third stage, which is already underway in some universities, is the full and complete institutional separation of research-intensive universities and teaching universities.

23. Oakeshott 1950, p.116, my emphasis.
24. Ibid., p.117. Jürgen Habermas, drawing on the tradition of German Idealism, expressed the same concerns somewhat more poetically: 'An institution remains capable of functioning only as long as it embodies in living form the idea inherent in it. As soon as the spirit leaves it, an institution rigidifies into something purely mechanical, as an organism without a soul decomposes into dead matter' (Habermas 1986, p.101).

5 The fourth mission

1. Oakeshott 1950, p.106. Collini suggests that 'Universities are organizations for the maintenance, extension, and transmission of intellectual enquiry', which amounts to much the same thing (Collini 2012, p.147).
2. Ibid., p.107. Maskell and Robinson put it even more simply: 'The aim, the objective and the goal of the university is just to be a university' (Maskell and Robinson 2001, p.93).
3. Deleuze and Guattari 1980, p.25.
4. Readings 1996, p.20.
5. University and College Union (retrieved from: http://www.ucu.org.uk/index.cfm?articleid=3672, 4 November 2011).
6. Academic freedom in the UK includes the right(s) to:
   • freedom in teaching and discussion;
   • freedom in carrying out research without commercial or political interference;
   • freedom to disseminate and publish one's research findings;
   • freedom from institutional censorship, including the right to express one's opinion publicly about the institution or the education system in which one works; and
   • freedom to participate in professional and representative academic bodies, including trade unions. (University and College Union, retrieved from: http://www.ucu.org.uk/ index.cfm?articleid=3672, 4 November 2011.)
   The educationalist Lewis Elton points out that, in Germany, academic freedom (*Lehrfreiheit*) is interpreted somewhat differently and also encompasses student learning (*Lernfreiheit*). Thus, the concept of *Lernfreiheit* includes 'the freedoms for students to switch courses and to fail', which he points out 'is totally foreign in the UK university system, which is increasingly tightly controlled, both from within and without' (Elton 2005, p.110).
7. University and College Union, op. cit.
8. Ibid.
9. Readings, op.cit., p.164, his emphasis.
10. Sennett 2008.
11. Bruce Macfarlane makes the point that these professional administrative roles are relatively new to the university, and that 'performing service roles, such as course co-ordinator, admissions tutor or head of department, used to be conceptualized

as part of the quid pro quo of academic life' (Macfarlane 2005, p.174). Anthony Smith and Frank Webster add: 'Once upon a time a head of a university would be an academic, chosen as the *primus inter pares* of a *collegium* of scholars. Today, the typical managerial figure in a university is the chief executive/vice chancellor on a six-figure salary, brandishing a strategic plan and without high-level academic achievements of his (still much less frequently her) own (Smith and Webster 1997, p.2).

12. Readings, op. cit., p.125.
13. Ibid., p.180.
14. Deleuze and Guattari, op. cit.
15. Colebrook 2002, pp.55–6.
16. In response to Oakeshott's assertion that 'a university is not a machine for achieving a particular purpose or producing a particular result', Deleuze and Guattari might have claimed that a university is comprised of numerous 'little machines', each with the potential to connect with other machines in networks and rhizomes in order to engage in specific projects (Deleuze and Guattari, op. cit., p.4).
17. Readings, op. cit., p.153, his emphasis.
18. Ibid., my emphasis.
19. Kinser 1998, p.13.
20. In a recent consultation paper on academic career pathways, my university has now expanded these 'career strands' to include teaching and scholarship; research; academic leadership, student support and internationalisation; and innovation and engagement.
21. As Readings points out, in the University of Excellence, the question of integration is no longer the concern of academics: 'All they have to do is get on with doing what they have always done, and the general question of integration will be resolved by the administration with the help of grids that chart the achievement of goals and tabulate efficiency' (Readings, op. cit., p.191).
22. For example, a recent report from the self-proclaimed 'liberal think-tank' *CentreForum* proposed the establishment of 'teaching only' universities. In a chapter entitled 'A new system which will tend to drive down prices', the author suggested that: 'Research strong institutions, which also have excellent teaching standards, would be officially classified as 'research' institutions. These institutions would (as they do now) undertake high quality research, teach students and award degrees. They would continue to be eligible to charge fees of up to £9,000 per year, and their students could access government subsidised fee and maintenance loans. The remaining institutions would become primarily teaching institutions, and as well as (or instead of) offering degrees of their own, would be able to teach towards accredited degrees validated by "research" institutions, or offer external degrees from other academic bodies (i.e. those that don't themselves teach)' (Wyness 2011, pp. 31–2). The report concludes: 'By employing staff dedicated to teaching, rather than research, and by condensing degrees into two year programs, it can be run at a cost that is sustainable and affordable in the long term. It puts students at the heart of the system – they can choose which degree, at which price, is right for them' (ibid., p.40).
23. For example, the *University and College of Football Business* in Burnley offers only three undergraduate degree courses in business-related aspects of football (http://www.ucfb.com/prospectus, accessed 17 December 2011). In the USA, McDonald's *Hamburger University* was established in 1961 and has been offering degree-level accreditation in all aspects of the fast-food business for many years.
24. Scott 1984, p.64.
25. Macfarlane, op. cit., pp.173–4.

26. See, for example, Elton 2001, 2005, 2008.
27. Elton 2005, p.108.
28. Humboldt 1810, cited and translated by Elton 2005, p.110. This is a somewhat eccentric translation, and differs significantly from the usually cited version, which renders the same passage as: 'One unique feature of higher intellectual institutions is that they conceive of science and scholarship as dealing with ultimately inexhaustible tasks: this means they are engaged in an unceasing process of inquiry' (Humboldt 1970, p.243, translated by E. Shils).
29. Elton 2005, op. cit., p.111.
30. Ibid., p.111.
31. Ibid., p.108.
32. Hughes 2005, p.16.
33. See, for example, Elton 2008.
34. Humboldt 1970, p.247.
35. Ibid., p.246.
36. Ibid., p.247.
37. Ibid., p.248.
38. Ibid., p.248.
39. Ibid., p.248, my emphasis. Maskell and Robinson approach the issue from the diametrically opposite position but still manage to arrive at the same conclusion. As they rather pithily put it: 'A way of downgrading a university is to turn it into a "teaching only" institution, that is, with no research going on: so "teaching" must be the irreducible basic university activity, to which "research" adds a touch of upmarket class' (Maskell and Robinson, op. cit., p.89).
40. Humboldt 1970, p.248. He continued by cautioning that, whilst academies were unnecessary, it was nevertheless important to retain 'the idea of an academy' in the form of its scholarly values, and, in particular, its function of 'subjecting the work of each member to the assessment of all the others' (ibid.).
41. Ibid., pp.247–8.
42. Elton 2005, op. cit., p.113.
43. Humboldt 1970, p.243.
44. Ibid., p.243.
45. See particularly Chapter 10, *The Scene of Teaching*, in Readings, op. cit., pp.150–65. However, Readings did not entirely subscribe to Humboldt's ideal of the student and teacher as partners in the common pursuit of knowledge. The problem for Readings was that if all thinking in the university begins from a commonly accepted starting point, it will inevitably also end in agreement. Thus 'it is a community whose dialogue is about nothing, in the sense that no issues for dispute are engaged. There are no differends, no radical and incommensurable differences, only arguments as to the exact nature of what it is that we agree on' (ibid., p.123).
46. Oakeshott, op. cit., p.116.
47. For example, The 'Russell Group' of the self-styled '20 major research-intensive universities of the UK' represents just 12 per cent of the higher education sector, and yet, as the group points out, 'the 2008 Research Assessment Exercise found that over 60% of the UK's very best ("world leading") research took place in Russell Group universities'. The group adds that 'The size and extent of Russell Group universities makes them *a prominent UK and international industry* in their own right:
    - They have a total economic output £22.3 billion per annum
    - They are responsible for supporting 243,000 jobs UK-wide
    - They are a major UK export industry, with overseas earnings of over £2 billion per annum.' (Russell Group 2012, my emphasis.)

48. Readings, op. cit., p.13.
49. Ibid., p.123.
50. Oakeshott, op. cit., p.106.

Part 3 Adventures in the paraversity

1. Derrida 1972, p.6.
2. Rorty 1989, p.9.
3. Ibid., p.9.

6 On the essay

1. Humboldt 1970, p.243.
2. Swansea University *Strategic Plan 2009–14.*
3. Lyotard 1979, p.5.
4. Charles Clarke's comments, cited in the previous chapter, bear restating here. The *Times Higher Education Supplement* reported on 9 May 2003 that: 'Education secretary Charles Clarke has again attacked learning for learning's sake by saying that the public purse should not fund "ornamental" subjects such as mediaeval history. Mr Clarke told a gathering at University College Worcester that he believed the state should pay only for higher education that had a "clear usefulness". This follows his earlier comments that studying classics is a waste of time.'
5. Lyotard, op. cit. The full title of the resulting book is *The Postmodern Condition: A Report on Knowledge.*
6. Ibid., p.5.
7. Ibid., p.20. Wittgenstein's concept of language games was examined in a little more detail in Chapter 2.
8. Of course, Francis Bacon made the same point over 400 years ago.
9. For example, Alain Badiou makes the distinction between the 'TV philosopher' who is wheeled out to answer questions on the issues of the day, and the 'genuine philosopher' who constructs her/his own problems and poses his/her own questions rather than merely resolving the problems of others (Badiou 2005).
10. For example, Derrida tells us that, from even before the time of Socrates ('he who does not write'), writing has been regarded merely as a 'supplement' to speech; speech has a presence and an immanence that can never fully be captured in the written word, which serves only as a record of what has been said (Derrida 1967a). This point will be examined further later in the chapter.
11. Lyotard, op. cit. Religious narratives are similarly self-legitimating.
12. Hence the adoption by almost all academic journals of the blind peer review, which promises an objective judgement based solely on the methodological merits of the paper, regardless of its author.
13. Ibid., p.25.
14. Barthes, 1957, p.96.
15. See, for example, Barthes's book, *Elements of Semiology*, particularly the section entitled 'Denotation and Connotation' (Barthes 1964b, pp.89–94).
16. Barthes 1967, p.4. The same year saw the publication by Jacques Derrida of a collection of extended essays entitled *Of Grammatology*, where grammatology was 'announced' as 'the science of writing' (Derrida, op. cit., p.4).
17. Barthes 1967, p.7. I will revisit Barthes's concept of the 'writer' later in this book.
18. Ibid., pp.7–8.

19. See, for example, *Writers, Intellectuals, Teachers* for an early statement of intent, and his later books such as *The Pleasure of the Text, Roland Barthes on Roland Barthes* and *A Lover's Discourse* for some striking examples.
20. Readings 1996, p.133.
21. Ibid., p.134.
22. Barthes 1971a, p.198.
23. van Manen 1990, p.127.
24. Or, as Barthes puts it: 'like a meteorite disappearing; it will *travel* far from my body' (Barthes 1971a, p.204).
25. Adorno 1958, p.108.
26. Ibid., p.110.
27. Good 1988, p.4.
28. Rorty 1989, p.8. Rorty's use of the word 'vocabulary' in this context might at first appear confusing. However, it is consistent with his broader point that whilst the world exists 'out there', 'truth' cannot exist independently of the human mind and is constructed and communicated through sentences. The words and syntax that we use to express and communicate these truths therefore, to some extent, shape the very things we are communicating.
29. Ibid., p.9.
30. Bloom 1973, p.94 – 'the meaning of a poem can only be another poem'.
31. Rorty, op. cit., p.9.
32. Ibid., p.9.
33. Deleuze and Guattari 1980.
34. Readings, op. cit., p.192.
35. Montaigne 1580, p.52.
36. This essay was extracted in slightly modified form from Gardner, L. and Rolfe, G. 'Essaying the essay: nursing scholarship and the hegemony of the laboratory', *Nurse Education Today*, in press.
37. Miller 2011.
38. Montaigne, op. cit., p.237.
39. Lukács, 1911.
40. Ibid., p.18.
41. Barthes 1966b.
42. Miller, op. cit.
43. Bakewell 2011, pp.7–8.
44. Good, op. cit., pp.4–5.
45. Ibid., p.6.
46. Ibid., p.6.
47. Whilst the issue of plagiarism is usually discussed in terms of poor scholarship and (in the case of students) cheating, there is an emerging subtext phrased in the language of the knowledge economy, that is, of plagiarism as the theft of intellectual property.
48. Adorno, op. cit., p.93.
49. Ibid., p.99.
50. Good, op.cit., p.178.
51. Ibid., p.1.
52. Montaigne, op. cit., p.52.
53. Adorno, op. cit., p.101.
54. Ibid., p.101.
55. Bense 1947, p.418.
56. Bakewell, op. cit., p.9.
57. Alter 2003.
58. Adorno, op. cit., p.106.

59. Barthes 1966a.
60. Good, op. cit., p.4.
61. Barthes, op. cit., p.4.
62. Adorno, op. cit., p.106.
63. Also, see Oakeshott's observation that 'the characteristic gift of a university is the gift of an interval' (Oakeshott 1950, pp.113–14). The notion of the university as a site of vocational training is still a recent one. As Krishnan Kumar pointed out in 1997, 'Universities are breathing spaces in life's course. They enable their members, young and old, to do things and to reflect on things for which the rest of their lives they will have neither the time nor the opportunity' (Kumar 1997, p.29). He continued: 'Universities are, or should be, different from other institutions. They should not train future doctors, lawyers, engineers, managers or even professional sociologists or economists ... This should be left to the professional schools and institutes, which are better able to do this, mixing the training where necessary with practical involvement' (ibid., p.31).
63. Lyotard 1983, p.149. Elsewhere, he expands on his notion of the enigmatic judgement, claiming that 'the thinker I am closest to in this regard is Aristotle, insofar as he recognizes ... that a judge worthy of the name has no true model to guide his judgements, and that the true nature of the judge is to pronounce judgements, and therefore prescriptions, just so, without criticism' (Lyotard and Thébaud 1979, p.26).
64. Several writers have remarked on the inability (perhaps the impossibility) of experts to articulate their judgements, including Michael Polanyi (tacit knowledge) and Hubert Dreyfus (intuitive expertise). And lest we forget, 'expert' (from the Latin *expertus* – to try out) is closely related to 'essay' (from the Latin *exagium* – to weigh, and the French *essayer* – to try).
65. Thus: 'In language there are only differences' (Saussure 1916, p.120).
66. For example: 'Languages are made to be spoken, writing serves only as a supplement to speech ... Thus the art of writing is nothing but a mediated representation of thought' (Rousseau 1782, cited in Derrida 1967a, p.144). 'Language and writing are two distinct systems of signs; the second exists for the sole purpose of representing the first' (Saussure, op. cit., cited in Derrida 1967a, p.30).
67. For example, *Force and Signification*, *Plato's Pharmacy*, and the extended essays published in *Of Grammatology* and *The Post Card*.
68. Barthes 1971a, p.190. Hélène Cixous puts it more poetically: 'But how is it that I do not speak that language of writing when I speak? I cannot write in the air with my voice? When I speak – no writing, only discourse' (Cixous 1998, p.149).
69. Derrida 1967b, p.12.
70. Ibid., p.11. Lyotard puts it thus: 'Generally speaking, writing is irresponsible, in the strict sense of the term, because it does not come in response to a question. It proceeds at its own pace. Montaigne is the absolute model here. Writing marches to its own beat and it has no debts' (Lyotard and Thébaud, op. cit., p.8).
71. Barthes 1966b.
72. Barthes 1975, p.56.
73. Cixous, op. cit., p.150.
74. Jabès 1959.
75. Jabès 1980, p.172.
76. Lyotard and Thébaud, op. cit., p.27.
77. Readings, op. cit., p.165.
78. Ibid., p.130.
79. Ibid., p.163.

7 On the seminar

1. In contrast, it will be recalled from a previous chapter that there is no reference to learning whatsoever in the mission statement of my own university.
2. Humboldt 1970, p. 243, my emphasis. Thus, Barthes is able to claim, citing Michelet, that 'I have always been careful to teach only what I did not know' (Barthes 1974, p.340).
3. Humboldt, op. cit, p.243. *Wissenschaft* has here been translated as 'science and scholarship', but it also has the meaning of 'higher learning'.
4. Ibid, p.243.
5. Kenny 1973, p.9.
6. Oakeshott 1950, p.113.
7. Leavis 1969, pp.65–6.
8. Ibid., p.66.
9. Elton 2005, p.113. Strictly speaking, this is not an entirely accurate analysis. In the sentence 'I teach mathematics', *mathematics* is the object of the verb *to teach*. In the sentence 'I teach students', *students* is the subject of the intransitive form of the verb (that is to say, the verb *to teach* here has no object).
10. Maskell and Robinson, 2001, p.90.
11. Freire 1972, pp.45–6. This approach to learning and teaching was also referred to by Carl Rogers as the 'mug and jug' model, where 'the faculty (the jug) possess the intellectual and factual knowledge and cause the student to be the passive recipient (the mug) so that the knowledge can be poured in' (Rogers 1983, p.187).
12. Freire, op. cit., p.45.
13. Ibid., p.46.
14. Rogers, op. cit., p.186.
15. Swansea University *Strategic Plan 2009–14.*
16. Hence the following shaggy dog story: A man walks into a pub and announces to everyone 'I taught my dog to whistle'. On hearing this, everyone becomes excited and demands to hear the dog whistle a tune, to which the man replies 'Unfortunately he never learned'.
17. Oakeshott 1972, p.67.
18. This is, perhaps, a somewhat less radical formulation than Bill Readings' assertion that 'the scene of teaching belongs to the sphere of justice rather than of truth' (Readings 1996, p.161).
19. Oakeshott 1965, pp. 45–6.
20. Ibid., p.49.
21. Ibid., p.51.
22. Ibid., p.57.
23. See Chapter 2.
24. Ibid., p.53.
25. Ibid., p.60.
26. Maskell and Robinson op.cit., p.91.
27. MacIntyre 1987, p.24.
28. Oakeshott 1965, p.60.
29. Ibid., p.61.
30. Freire, op.cit., p.56.
31. See, for example, Holquist 2002.
32. Freire, op. cit., p.81.
33. Readings, op. cit., p.155.
34. Ibid., p.156.
35. Ibid., p.156.

36. Ibid., p.158, his emphasis.
37. Barthes 1974, p.332.
38. Ibid., p.333.
39. Ibid., p.333.
40. Barthes 1971a, p.190.
41. Ibid., p.190, his emphasis.
42. Barthes 1974, p.333.
43. Ibid., p.334, his emphasis.
44. Readings, op. cit., p.192.
45. Barthes 1974, p.336.
46. Ibid., p.336, his emphasis.
47. Oakeshott 1965, p.61.
48. Barthes, op. cit., p.337.
49. Rogers 1969, p.165.
50. Knowles *et al.* 2005, p.64.
51. Freire, op. cit., pp.56–7, his emphasis.
52. Rogers 1983, p.103.
53. Barthes 1974, p.337, his emphasis. 'Disappointed' might appear to be a curious word to use in this context. However, its literal meaning as dis-appointed might be better understood as *un-appointed*. That is to say, the practice of teaching is removed or taken out of the seminar.

8 On the book

1. Collini 2012, p.147.
2. Ibid., p.147. Collini was actually making this claim for the university, but it applies equally well to the book.
3. See the epigraph to this chapter. Whilst I accept that Cage's story is most likely an exaggeration, if not an allegory, it is nevertheless interesting to speculate on the identity of the 'book written by an author whose name began with Z' that earned Cage the highest grade in class.
4. Although written in 1941, it is possible to see in this story a foreshadowing of some of the problems currently being encountered as a result of the ever-growing cache of knowledge, facts and trivia to be found on the internet.
5. Deleuze and Guattari 1980, p.4.
6. Ibid., p.4.
7. Ibid., p.5.
8. Ibid., p.12.
9. Ibid., p.11.
10. Ibid., p.12, their emphasis.
11. Barthes 1971b, pp.156–7.
12. Ibid., p.161.
13. Ibid., pp.156–7, his emphasis.
14. Ibid., p.157.
15. Barthes 1968, p.145.
16. Barthes 1973, p.4.
17. Barthes 1971b, p.159.
18. Barthes 1968, p.146.
19. Barthes 1971b, p.160.
20. Barthes 1968, p.148.
21. Weinberger 1999, p.xi.
22. Borges 1941, p.13, my emphasis. Unless stated otherwise, all references to Borges's work are taken from *Fictions*, his first collection of short stories.

23. Borges 1939a.
24. It is important to understand the difference between 'fictional' and 'fictitious'. 'Fictional' means simply 'from fiction', which in turn is derived from the Latin *fingere*, meaning to shape or construct. The word 'fictional' therefore means 'made up' or fabricated and has no connotation of either truth or falsehood; a fictional story is perfectly capable of conveying truth. 'Fictitious', on the other hand, means false or feigned. A fictional story is a made up story; a fictitious story is a false one.
25. Barthes 1968, p.55.
26. Borges 1942, p.231.
27. Derrida 1967a, p.158. Derrida's phrase 'il n'y a pas de hors-text' is sometimes translated as 'there is nothing outside the text', but is perhaps more accurately rendered as 'there is no *outside-text*'.
28. Derrida 1979, p.81.
29. Derrida 1967a, p.152.
30. Spivak 1974, p.lxxvii.
31. http://blog.johnath.com/2006/11/15/celestial-emporium-of-benevolent-knowledge/. Kuhn, it appears, really was a translator of Chinese texts, and was presumably cited by Borges in order to add some authenticity to his account of the Celestial Emporium. The effectiveness of this attempt to blur fact and fiction can be seen from an entry to the website *Linguist List* (operated by the Institute for Language Information and Technology (ILIT) at Eastern Michigan University) by Laszlo Cseresnyesi, Professor of Linguistics at Shikoku Gakuin University: 'First, I assumed that this must have been a Borgesian joke, as we (i.e. my Chinese colleagues and myself) had been unable to find any encyclopedia whose title may have been rendered in English as the Celestial Emporium of Benevolent Knowledge. However, Borges referred to Franz Kuhn (1884–1961), whose work I have been familiar with. Franz Kuhn was a renowned translator and scholar of Chinese literature. Since I knew that Franz Kuhn was real, I felt I should assume that the Chinese encyclopedia was also genuine' (http://linguistlist.org/issues/7/7-1446.html).
32. According to some accounts, the radio broadcast in docudrama form by Orson Welles of his namesake's novel *The War of the Worlds* was taken by some to be a live account of an actual Martian invasion, thereby causing a certain amount of panic on the streets of America. However, its effects were short-lived.
33. Borges 1975, p.87.
34. Ibid., p.88. Bikaner, in true Borgesian fashion, is a real place in northern India.
35. Ibid., p.88.
36. Ibid., p.89.
37. This, as Borges suggests, is a variation on the theme of the monkeys with typewriters who, given enough time, would produce the complete works of Shakespeare. Borges rather drolly points out that 'strictly speaking, one immortal monkey would be sufficient' (Borges 1939b, p.215).
38. Ibid., p.216.
39. Borges 1941, p.78.
40. Readings 1991, p.xxv, my emphasis.
41. Ibid., p.xxv.
42. Readings 1996, p.192.
43. Derrida 1992b, p.197.

References

Adorno, T.W. (1947) *Dialectic of Enlightenment*. Verso, London, 1979 (trans. J. Cumming).

Adorno, T.W. (1951) 'Cultural criticism and society', in *Prisms*. MIT Press, Cambridge, MA: pp.17–34.

Adorno, T.W. (1958) 'The essay as form', in B. O'Connor (ed.) *The Adorno Reader*. Blackwell, Oxford, 2000, pp.91–111.

Adorno, T.W. (1962) 'Why Philosophy?', in *Man and Philosophy*. Max Huber Verlag, Munich (trans. M.D. Senft-Howie and W. Leifer), pp.11–24.

Adorno, T.W. (1966) *Negative Dialectics*. Routledge, London, 1973 (trans. E.B. Ashton).

Alter, N.M. (2003) 'Memory essays', in U. Biermann (ed.) *Stuff It: The Video Essay in the Digital Age*. Edition Voldemeer, Zurich, pp.12–23.

Andreson, L.W. (2000) 'A useable transdisciplinary conception of scholarship', *Higher Education Research and Development*, 19, 2, 137–55.

Badiou, A. (2005) 'Thinking the event', in P. Engelmann (ed.) *Philosophy in the Present*. Polity Press, London 2009 (trans. P. Thomas and A. Toscano), pp.1–48.

Badiou, A. (2009) *Second Manifesto for Philosophy*. Polity Press, London, 2011 (trans. L. Burchill).

Bakewell, D. (2011) *How to Live: A life of Montaigne*. Vintage, London.

Barnett, R. (2000) *Realizing the University in an Age of Supercomplexity*. Open University Press, Buckingham.

Barnett, R. (2005) *Reshaping the University*. Open University Press, Maidenhead.

Barthes, R. (1957) 'Myth today', in Susan Sontag (ed.) *A Roland Barthes Reader*. Vintage, London, 1982, pp.93–149.

Barthes, R. (1963) *Sur Racine*. Éditions de Seuil, Paris.

Barthes, R. (1964a) *Essais Critiques*. Éditions de Seuil, Paris.

Barthes, R. (1964b) *Elements of Semiology*. Hill and Wang, New York, 1973 (trans. A. Lavers and C. Smith).

Barthes, R. (1966a) *Criticism and Truth*. Continuum, London, 1987 (trans. K.P. Keuneman).

Barthes, R. (1966b) 'To write: an intransitive verb?' in *The Rustle of Language*. University of California Press, Berkeley and Los Angeles, 1989 (trans. R. Howard), pp.11–21.

Barthes, R. (1967) 'From science to literature', in *The Rustle of Language*. University of California Press, Berkeley and Los Angeles, 1989 (trans. R. Howard), pp.3–10.

Barthes, R. (1968) 'The death of the author', in *Image Music Text*. Fontana, London, 1977 (trans. S. Heath), pp.142–8.

Barthes, R. (1971a) 'Writers, intellectuals, teachers', in *Image, Music Text*. Fontana, London, 1977 (trans. S. Heath), pp.190–215.

Barthes, R. (1971b) 'From work to text', in *Image, Music Text*. Fontana, London, 1977 (trans. S. Heath), pp.155–64.

Barthes, R. (1973) *S/Z*. Blackwell, Oxford, 1974 (trans. Richard Miller).

Barthes, R. (1974) 'To the seminar', in *The Rustle of Language*. University of California Press, Berkeley and Los Angeles, 1989 (trans. R. Howard), pp.332–42.

Barthes, R. (1975) *Roland Barthes by Roland Barthes*. Macmillan, Basingstoke, 1995 (trans. Richard Howard).

Barthes, R. (1977) 'Inaugural lecture', in Susan Sontag (ed.) *A Roland Barthes Reader*, 1982. Vintage, London, pp.457–78.

Bauman, Z. (1997) 'Universities: old, new and different', in A. Smith and F. Webster (eds) *The Postmodern University? Contested Visions of Higher Education in Society*. Open University Press, Buckingham, pp.17–26.

Bense, M. (1947) 'Über den Essay und seine Prose'. *Merkur*, 1, 3, 414–24.

Bloom, H. (1973) *The Anxiety of Influence*. Oxford University Press, Oxford.

Borges, J.L. (1939a) 'When fiction lives in fiction', in J.L. Borges *The Total Library: Non-Fiction 1922–1986*. Penguin Books, Harmondsworth, 1999, pp.160–2.

Borges, J.L. (1939b) 'The total library', in J.L. Borges *The Total Library: Non-Fiction 1922–1986*. Penguin Books, Harmondsworth, 1999, pp.214–16.

Borges, J.L. (1941) *Fictions*. Jupiter Books, London, 1965.

Borges, J.L. (1942) 'John Wilkins' analytical language', in J.L. Borges *The Total Library: Non-Fiction 1922–1986*. Penguin Books, Harmondsworth, 1999, pp.227–32.

Borges, J.L. (1975) *The Book of Sand*. Penguin Books, Harmondsworth.

Boyer, E.L. (1990) *Scholarship Reconsidered*. The Carnegie Foundation for the Advancement of Teaching. Princeton, New Jersey.

Brewer, D. (2008) *The Enlightenment Past*. Cambridge University Press, Cambridge.

Cixous, H. (1998) *Stigmata: Escaping Texts*. Routledge, London.

Colebrook, C. (2002) *Gilles Deleuze*. Routledge, London.

Collini, S. (2012) *What Are Universities For?* Penguin Books, London.

Comte, A. (1830) *Introduction to Positive Philosophy*. Hackett Publishing Company, Indianapolis, 1988 (trans. F. Ferré).

Deleuze, G. and Guatarri, F. (1980) *A Thousand Plateaus*. University of Minnesota Press, Minneapolis, 1989 (trans. B. Massumi).

Department for Education (1993) *'Higher quality and choice'; The Charter for Higher Education*. Department for Education, London.

Department for Education and Skills (2003) *The Future of Higher Education: Creating Opportunity, Releasing Potential, Achieving Excellence*. The Stationery Office, London.

Department of Trade and Industry (2000) *Excellence and Opportunity: A Science and Innovation Policy for the 21st Century*. Office of Science and Technology, London.

Derrida, J. (1967a) *Of Grammatology*. Johns Hopkins University Press, Baltimore, MD, 1976 (trans. G.C. Spivak).

Derrida, J. (1967b) 'Force and signification', in J. Derrida, *Writing and Difference*. Routledge, London, 1978 (trans. Alan Bass), pp.3–30.

Derrida, J. (1972) *Dissemination*. Continuum, London, 2004 (trans. Barbara Johnson).

Derrida, J. (1979) 'Living on/border lines', in H. Bloom *et al. Deconstructionism and Criticism*. Seabury Press, New York, 1979 (trans. James Hulbert), pp.75–176.

Derrida, J. (1987) 'Ulysses gramophone: hear say yes in Joyce', in P. Kamuf (ed.) *A Derrida Reader: Between the Blinds*. Harvester Wheatsheaf, New York, 1991, pp.571–98.

Derrida, J. (1992a) *Demeure: Fiction and Testimony*. Stanford University Press, California, 2000 (trans. E. Rottenberg).

Derrida, J. (1992b) *Afterwords*. Outside Books, Tampere, Finland.

Derrida, J. (1996) 'As if I were dead: an interview with Jacques Derrida', in J. Brannigan, R. Robbins and J. Wolfreys (eds) *Applying: To Derrida*. Macmillan, Basingstoke, pp.212–26.

Drucker, P.F. (1994) 'The age of social transformation'. *The Atlantic Monthly*, 274, 5, 53–80.

Eagleton, T. (1996) *The Function of Criticism*. Verso, London.

Elam, D. (1996) 'Foreword', in B. Readings, *The University in Ruins*. Harvard University Press, Cambridge, MA.

Elton, L. (2001) 'Research and teaching: conditions for a positive link' [1]. *Teaching in Higher Education*, 6, 43–56.

Elton, L. (2005) 'Scholarship and the research and teaching nexus', in R. Barnett (ed.) *Reshaping the University*. Open University Press, Maidenhead, pp.108–18.

Elton, L. (2008) 'Collegiality and complexity: Humboldt's relevance to British universities today'. *Higher Education Quarterly*, 62, 3, 224–36.

Fernandez-Armesto, F. (1997) *Truth: A History and Guide for the Perplexed*. Bantam Press, London.

Forscher, B. (1963) 'Letter to the editor'. *Science*, 142, 339.

Foucault, M. (1978) 'What is critique?' in Sylvère Lotinger (ed.), *The Politics of Truth*. Semiotext(e), Los Angeles, CA, 2007, pp.41–82.

Foucault, M. (1981) 'Practicing criticism,' or 'Is it really important to think?'. In Lawrence Kritzman (ed.), *Foucault, Politics, Philosophy, Culture*. Routledge, New York and London, 1988, pp.152–6.

Freire, P. (1972) *Pedagogy of the Oppressed*. Penguin, Harmondsworth (trans. Myra Bergman Ramos).

Furedi, F. (2004) *Where Have All the Intellectuals Gone?* Continuum, London.

Gibbons, M., Limoges, C., Nowotny, H., Schwartzman, S., Scott, P. and Trow, M. (1994) *The New Production of Knowledge*. Sage, London.

Good, G. (1988) *The Observing Self: Rediscovering the Essay*. Routledge, London.

Graham, G. (2008) *Universities: The Recovery of an Idea*, Imprint Academic, Exeter.

Habermas, J. (1968) *Knowledge and Human Interest*. Polity Press, Cambridge, 1987 (trans. J.J. Shapiro).

Habermas, J. (1986) 'The idea of the university: learning processes', in S.W. Nicholsen (ed.) *The New Conservatism: Cultural Criticism and the Historians' Debate*. Polity Press, Cambridge, 1989 (trans. S.W. Nicholsen), pp.100–27.

HEFCE (2006) *RAE 2008 Panel Criteria and Working Methods, Annex 3*. http://www.rae.ac.uk/pubs/2006/01/docs/annexes.pdf

Heidegger, M. (1938) 'The age of the world picture', in *The Question Concerning*

Technology and Other Essays. Harper & Row, New York, 1978 (trans. W. Lovitt), pp.115–54.

Heidegger, M. (1951) 'Building dwelling thinking', in D.F. Krell (ed.) *Basic Writings: Martin Heidegger*, Routledge, London, 1993, pp.343–64.

Heidegger, M. (1955) *Discourse on Thinking*. Harper & Row, New York, 1969 (trans. J.M. Anderson).

Holquist, M. (2002) *Dialogism*. Routledge, London.

Hughes, M. (2005) 'The mythology of research and teaching relationships', in R. Barnett (ed.) *Reshaping the University*. Open University Press, Maidenhead, pp.14–26.

Humboldt, W. von (1810) 'Über die innere und äußere Organisation der höheren wissenschaftlichen Anstalten in Berlin', in H. Weinstock (ed.) *Wilhelm von Humboldt*. Fischer Bücherei, Frankfurt, 1957, pp.126–34.

Humboldt, W. von (1970) 'On the spirit and organisational framework of intellectual institutions in Berlin'. *Minerva*, 8, 242–67 (trans. E. Shils).

Jabès, E. (1959) *Je Bâtis ma Demeure (Poèmes 1943–57)*. Gallimard, Paris.

Jabès, E. (1980) 'The pre-existence of the last book', in *From the Book to the Book: An Edmond Jabès Reader*. Wesleyan University Press, Hanover, 1991 (trans. Rosemarie Waldrop), pp.172–5.

Jaspers, K. (1923) *Die Idee der Universität [The Idea of the University]*, Springer, Berlin.

Kant, I. (1787) *Critique of Pure Reason*. Macmillan, London, 1929 (trans. N. Kemp Smith).

Kant, I. (1798) *The Conflict of the Faculties*, University of Nebraska Press, Lincoln, NE, 1992 (trans. M.J. Gregor).

Kenny, A. (1973) *Wittgenstein*. Allen Lane, London.

Kerr, C. (1963) *The Uses of the University*. Harvard University Press, Cambridge, MA.

Kinser, K. (1998) 'Faculty at private for-profit universities: the University of Phoenix as a new model?' *International Higher Education*, 13 (Fall), 13–14.

Knowles, M.S., Elwood, F.H. and Swanson, R.A. (2005) *The Adult Learner*. Elsevier, London.

Kumar, K. (1997) 'The need for place', in A. Smith and F. Webster (eds) *The Postmodern University? Contested Visions of Higher Education in Society*. Open University Press, Buckingham, pp.27–35.

Leavis, F.R. (1969) *English Literature in Our Time and the University*. Cambridge University Press, Cambridge.

Lukács, G. (1911) 'On the nature and form of the essay', in *Soul and Form*. MIT Press, Cambridge, MA, 1978 (trans. A. Bostock), pp.16–34.

Lyotard, J.-F. (1979) *The Postmodern Condition: A Report on Knowledge*. Manchester University Press, Manchester, 1984 (trans. G. Bennington and B. Massumi).

Lyotard, J.-F. (1983) *The Differend: Phrases in Dispute*. University of Minnesota Press, Minneapolis, MN, 1988 (trans. G. Van Den Abbeele).

Lyotard, J.-F. (1987) 'Rewriting modernity'. *SubStance*, 54.

Lyotard, J.-F. and Thébaud, J.-L. (1979) *Just Gaming*. University of Minnesota Press, Minneapolis, MN, 1985 (trans. Wlad Godzich).

Macfarlane, B. (2005) 'Placing service in academic life', in R. Barnett (ed.) *Reshaping the University*. Open University Press, Maidenhead, pp.165–77.

MacIntyre, A. (1987) 'The idea of an educated public', in G. Haydon (ed.)

Education and Values: The Richard Peters Lectures. University of London Institute of Education, London, pp.15–36.

Maskell, D. and Robinson, I. (2001) *The New Idea of a University.* Haven Books, London.

Melody, W. (1997) 'Universities and public policy', in A. Smith and F. Webster (eds) *The Postmodern University? Contested Visions of Higher Education in Society.* Open University Press, Buckingham, pp.72–84.

Mill, J.S. (1833) 'A few observations on the French Revolution', in J.S. Mill *Dissertations and Discussions* (Vol. 1). John W. Parker and Son, London, 1859, pp.56–62.

Miller, L. (2011) 'An Essay on the essay'. www.nottinghilleditions.com/journal2011

Mills, C.W. (1959) *The Sociological Imagination.* Penguin, Harmondsworth.

Montaigne, M. de (1580) 'Of repentance', in D.M. Frame (ed.) *The Complete Essays of Montaigne.* Everyman, London, 2005 (trans. Donald M. Frame), pp.909–21.

Nancy, J.-L. (1996) *Being Singular Plural.* Stanford University Press, CA, 2000, (trans. R.D. Richardson and A.E. O'Byrne).

National Committee of Inquiry into Higher Education (1997) *Higher Education in the Learning Society: Report of the National Committee.* HMSO, London.

Newman, J.H. (1858) *The Idea of a University.* University of Notre-Dame Press, IN, 1892.

Oakeshott, M. (1950) 'The idea of a university', in M. Oakeshott, *The Voice of Liberal Learning.* Liberty Fund, Indianapolis, IN, 2001, pp.105–17.

Oakeshott, M. (1965) 'Learning and teaching', in M. Oakeshott, *The Voice of Liberal Learning.* Liberty Fund, Indianapolis, IN, 2001, pp.35–61.

Oakeshott, M. (1972) 'Education: the engagement and its frustration', in M. Oakeshott, *The Voice of Liberal Learning.* Liberty Fund, Indianapolis, IN, 2001, pp.62–104.

Panagia, D. (2010) '"Partage du sensible": the distribution of the sensible', in J.-P. Deranty (ed.) *Jacques Rancière: Key Concepts.* Acumen, Durham, pp.95–103.

Picard, R. (1965) *Nouvelle Critique ou Nouvelle Imposture.* Pauvert, Utrecht.

Quality Assurance Agency for Higher Education (2000) *Handbook for Academic Review,* QAAHE, Gloucester.

Readings, B. (1991) *Introducing Lyotard: Art and Politics.* Routledge, London.

Readings, B. (1996) *The University in Ruins.* Harvard University Press, Cambridge, MA.

Ritzer, G. (2004) *The McDonaldization of Society,* revised edn, Sage, Thousand Oaks, CA.

Robbins, Lord (1963) *Higher Education: Report of the Committee Appointed by the Prime Minister under the Chairmanship of Lord Robbins.* HMSO, London.

Rogers, C. (1969) *Freedom to Learn: A View of what Education might Become,* Charles Merrill, Columbus, OH.

Rogers, C. (1983) *Freedom to learn for the 80s.* Merrill, Columbus, OH.

Roper, C.D. (2005) *Extension, Outreach, Knowledge Transfer, Technology Transfer: What Is It that We Do – Officially?* Paper presented at Association of Leadership Education 2005 Annual Conference. http://www.leadershipeducators.org/Resources/Documents/Conferences/Wilmington/roper.pdf

Rorty, R. (1989) *Contingency, Irony and Solidarity.* Cambridge University Press, Cambridge.

Russell   Group   (2012)   *Research   at   Russell   Group   Universities.*
    http://www.russellgroup.ac.uk/research

Saussure, F. de (1916) *Course in General Linguistics.* McGraw-Hill, New York, 1966
    (trans. W. Baskin).

Schlegel, F. (1841) *Lectures on the History of Literature, Ancient and Modern.* Smith
    and Wright, New York.

Scott, P. (1984) *The Crisis of the University.* Croom Helm, London.

Scruton, R. (2004) 'Review of *Where Have All the Intellectuals Gone?*' by Frank
    Furedi. *The Times,* 4 September 2004.

Sennett, R. (2008) *The Craftsman.* Penguin Books, London.

Smith, A. and Webster, F. (1997) 'Changing ideas of the university', in A. Smith and
    F. Webster (eds) *The Postmodern University? Contested Visions of Higher Education
    in Society.* Open University Press, Buckingham, pp.1–14.

Smith, B. (1994) *European Philosophy and the American Academy.* The Hegeler
    Institute, La Salle, IL.

Smith, B. *et al.* (1992) 'Open letter against Derrida receiving an honorary doctorate
    from Cambridge University'. *The Times* [London], 9 May.

Snow, C.P. (1959) *The Two Cultures.* Cambridge University Press, Cambridge.

Sokal, A. and Bricmont, J. (1998) *Intellectual Impostures.* Profile Books, London.

Sorell, T. (1991) *Scientism: Philosophy and the Infatuation with Science,* Routledge,
    London.

Spivak, G.C. (1974) 'Translator's preface', in J. Derrida, *Of Grammatology* (1967).
    Johns Hopkins University Press, Baltimore, MD, 1976.

Swansea University, *Strategic Plan 2009–14.* www.swansea.ac.uk/media/
    media,40519,en.pdf

Tallis, R. (2000) 'Evidence-based and evidence-free generalisations', in M. Grant
    (ed.) *The Raymond Tallis Reader.* Palgrave, Basingstoke, pp.309–29.

University Grants Committee (1958) *University Development 1952–1957.* Cmd 534.
    HMSO, London.

Usher, R. (2002) 'A diversity of doctorates: fitness for the knowledge economy?'
    Higher Education Research and Development, 21, 2, 143–53.

van Manen, M. (1990) *Researching Lived Experience,* 2nd edn. Althouse Press,
    Ontario, 1997.

Weinberger, E. (1999) 'A note on this edition', in J.L. Borges *The Total Library:
    Non-Fiction 1922–1986.* Penguin Books, Harmondsworth, 1999, pp.xi–xvi.

Wittgenstein, L. (1922) *Tractatus Logico-Philosophicus.* Routledge, London, 1974.

Wittgenstein, L. (1953) *Philosophical Investigations.* Basil Blackwell, Oxford, 1972.

Wyness, G. (2011) *Degrees of Quality: How to Deliver the Courses we Need at Prices we
    can Afford,* CentreForum, London.

Žižek, S. (2005) 'Philosophy is not a dialogue', in P. Engelmann (ed.) *Philosophy in
    the Present.* Polity Press, London, 2009 (trans. P. Thomas and A. Toscano),
    pp.49–72.

Index